Strength for Living

LEONARD SANDERSON

BROADMAN PRESS
Nashville, Tennessee

To the memory of Reverend L. G. Frey
my boyhood pastor and long-time co-worker

Preface

Everybody is interested in strength for living. Advertisers coin catchy phrases and paint colorful pictures about "luxurious living," "comfortable living," and "easy living."

People spend most of their time "making a living" and most of what they make "living it up." There is magic in words like: family living, healthful living, Christian living, suburban living, country living, happy living, or "just plain" living.

It is the nature of life to desire to live long and well. It is characteristic of all living things to fight to live. Chop down a tree and a sprout appears on the old stump. Budding and grafting are successful because of this characteristic. Cut off the extremities of some animals and new ones replace them. Apply insecticide and after a while the insect develops resistance to it.

Only human beings, so far as we know, discuss life, research it, plan it, study it and prolong it by deliberation and organization.

The sophisticated become excited and the naive become fearful when the scientist talks about "creating" life in the test tube. The mystery and mastery of life are the motivating influence in reading books, watching plays, exploring planets, forming governments, getting married, going to church, studying medicine *ad infinitum*.

The Bible is exceedingly vibrant on the subject. Refer to a good Bible concordance, and you will find over 400 times where the word life is used in the English translations, not to mention the almost countless allusions to the subject by the use of other words.

Two passages of Scripture, both found in the same chapter of Philippians (4:13,19), provide the inspiration for this series of messages. Quite naturally, this is because these passages have provided the writer with strength for living.

My first thought was to tell you "my experience" at this point. I then decided that, though the messages were motivated by "my experience" I will simply let the personal testimony "overflow" wherever and whenever the water level reaches the level of the spillway.

Some two years after these passages had come to wield so much influence in my life, the manager of the local telegraph office said: "I think I could guess your favorite Bible verses. You use Philippians 4:13 and 19 in most of your telegrams."

Preachers preach, teachers teach, and Christians witness on the basis of what Christ means to them in their own experience. Witnessing is not merely a matter of telling people how to become a Christian. It is more a matter of demonstrating the result of becoming a Christian.

"Life" is a word used to describe salvation in Christ Jesus. It is sometimes referred to as "eternal life." Now eternal life is not something altogether in the future. Jesus talked to a prominent Jew about being "born again." Paul wrote about new life. This new life begins at the time of the new birth. It continues as long as we live in this world as well as in the world to come. Strength for living is something we need both in this life and in the life to come. The promises of our Lord apply to this life as well as to life beyond.

More and more I have asked myself the question: Why do I believe the promises of Jesus when he tells me about life after death if I do not believe his promises concerning what he will do for me before death? Do I just trust him for "eternal life" because that is more remote but do not trust him for daily strength for living because of the stark realities that stare me in the face today? As I faced these questions in my own life and found assurance in the Scriptures and in experience, it began to influence my evangelistic ministry.

Pretty soon I found that people respond to a message concerning what Jesus offers *now*. It is pretty difficult to get the attention of some people concerning Jesus' ability to save them from a hell to come when they are living in a literal hell right now. They seem to figure that if they can get through this present hell, maybe they will have a little more time to prepare for the hell to come. When people learn that Jesus can save them from the hell of this world as well as the world to come, they are able to accept both promises more easily.

These chapters are basically evangelistic. The emphasis is upon the evangelization of the total person for the present and for all the future. It is my conviction that this is the emphasis of Jesus in the entire New Testament. These chapters, I hope, will be helpful to a person in his search for strength for living regardless of his religious background or experience. If you are not a Christian, it is hoped that you will find the one who gives strength for living. If you are a Christian already, it is hoped that these chapters will help you to draw on the account which our Lord has already deposited in your name.

Contents

1. Strength for Living   9
2. People Are Important   16
3. What God Can Do   25
4. Strength for Temptation   33
5. Strength for the Home   44
6. Personal Strength   52
7. Strength for Witness   63
8. How to Be Sure   75
9. How to Be Happy   87
10. How to Be Holy   95
11. How to Be Humble   107
12. When Life Begins   118

1

Strength for Living

A pastor answered the telephone early one morning.

"Pastor," said the church member on the other end of the line, "I apologize for calling you at this time of day, but I need your help. My brother from out of town is visiting me, and he is about to go to pieces. He was up all night walking the floor. He has taken I-don't-know-how-many tranquilizers, but he just can't relax. I just wondered if you would come over and talk to him?"

"I'll be glad to," the pastor responded, "but do you know anything about what is causing your brother's anxiety?"

"Yes, I know what it is. My brother has done very well in his business. He has saved some money and made some good investments, but apparently he has made the mistake of putting too many eggs in one basket. It looks like he is about to lose $500,000.00 in one oil deal in a midwestern state. He is about to lose his mind. Can you help him?"

The pastor thought this was a pretty big deal for a preacher to tackle so early in the morning, but he said,

"I'll be right over as soon as I get dressed."

When the pastor arrived and tried to make some small talk to ease the tension, the visiting brother said, "Preacher, I am in trouble. I wouldn't worry about this myself. I'd forget it. I can live on my pension, but the money is for my son. He has gotten his master's degree and is ready to start out on his own. This money would set him up. He is not the kind of boy who can start from scratch. He has been my life for twenty-five years. This is what I have been living for. Now everything has caved in. If I lose this money, we are ruined."

The pastor didn't get very far with the idea that this might be just the making of the boy. The challenge might be the needed inspiration to really apply himself to making a future. The father was impatient at this very suggestion.

The pastor then talked with the man about his own life. He said he was a Christian. As a boy, he had professed faith in Christ and joined the little home church in the country. That his Christian life was only nominal was illustrated by the fact that he had never been to church much. He guessed he was still a member of the old home church.

"Do you believe the Bible, Mr. ————?" asked the pastor.

"Yes, I believe the Bible, but it doesn't say anything about a situation like mine, does it?"

"Mr. ————," asked the pastor, "if you read a passage in the Bible where God promises to help you with your problem, would you take it at face value and turn it over to the Lord?"

"Y-yes," said the man, his expression revealing his doubt.

The pastor took a New Testament from his pocket and

said, "Let's look at two Scriptures right in the same chapter." He opened the New Testament to the fourth chapter of Philippians. Sitting beside the man on the couch, the pastor pointed to verse 13. It read, "I can do all things through Christ which strengtheneth me."

"Do you believe this?" the pastor asked.

"Oh yes, I believe the Bible."

"Well, it says right here that he will give you the necessary strength for anything."

"Well, that's what I need—but I just don't know."

"Now here is another verse." The pastor pointed to verse 19 as he held the Bible for the man to see. At this point, the man took the Bible in his own hands and read silently. The pastor quoted the words aloud as the man looked at them, "But my God shall supply all your need according to his riches in glory by Christ Jesus."

"Who is it, Mr. ———, who will supply all your need?" asked the pastor as he pointed to the word, "God."

"It says God will."

"How much of your need does he promise to supply?" asked the pastor.

"It says every need but," he squirmed on the couch, "I just don't know. I've just had bad luck I guess." The pastor, remembering an experience he had read about, said, "Mr. ———, do you have your checkbook with you?" The man looked rather perplexed. "Yes, I have a checkbook."

"Would you lend me a blank check?" This was before the present requirement by banks for personalized checks.

The man, now thinking the pastor must be more deranged than himself, tore out a blank check and gave it to the pastor.

"How do you usually sign your name?" the pastor asked.

"I beg your pardon?"

"How do you usually sign your name in business transactions?"

The man told him, and the pastor began filling in the check, writing the man's name on the face of the check.

"The next thing on the blank check, after your name, is the amount of the check. Now, since you believe God will keep his promise to meet every need of yours, what is your real need? Just suppose God is writing a check. What is your need?"

The man hesitated. He could not say he just had to have this half million dollars. Neither would he say that if he had the half million, he would have no other need.

One of our weaknesses in praying is at this point. It is much easier to pray in broad generalities. It won't be as embarrassing if we fail, and we really expect to fail. Jesus said, "If ye shall ask any thing in my name, I will do it" (John 14:14).

Do you believe Jesus can keep this promise? Do you believe he will do what he says he will? Then ask for it specifically. This is not irreverent, if you ask in Jesus' name. Rather, it is irreverent if you do not.

However, because of the particular difficulty which the man faced and because God knew his real need, the pastor and the worried man agreed that they would let (X) represent the need. So they wrote on the check, "$XXXXX.-xx." They wanted to be sure it was well covered. Then on the check, in the space reserved for the amount, the pastor filled in: "All your need."

"Do you believe," asked the pastor, "that God can meet all your need? Does he have the resources? The Bible says,

'The earth is the Lord's, and the fulness thereof; the world, and they that dwell therein. For he hath founded it upon the seas, and established it upon the floods' (Psalm 24: 1-2). 'For every beast of the forest is mine, and the cattle upon a thousand hills. . . . for the world is mine, and the fulness thereof' " (Psalm 50:10,12).

Now if the Lord owns the cattle on a thousand hills, he owns all the natural resources on the earth and those beneath the surface of the earth. He owns the banks and the businesses, the factories and the foodstuffs. He owns all the vast explored and unexplored planets in space. He possesses this universe and perhaps other universes we do not know about.

While in an evangelistic crusade in a church in Tulsa, Oklahoma, I was out making calls one afternoon with a young businessman. As we passed by a beautiful new office building, I remarked, "That is a magnificent building."

He said, "Yes, that belongs to my father."

"Sure enough," I said. "You have every reason to be proud of that."

I referred to some other nice property during the afternoon, and each time the young businessman said, "That belongs to my father, too."

I said, "You are not pulling my leg, are you?"

He said, "No, I'm not kidding you, preacher. God is my father and he owns everything." I felt embarrassed.

Do you believe this? It sure relieves a lot of pressure when you are worried about things. If it all belongs to the Lord, he can transfer title or use any time he wills. All I have to do is stay in his will.

The anxious man began to understand what the pastor was reading from the Bible.

"Who signs the check?" he asked with a smile. The smile revealed some progress.

"Let's look back at the passage to see who signs the check," said the pastor, as he pointed to the words, "by Christ Jesus." Jesus signs the check. He is the one who has an account in heaven. The only account I have in heaven is in Jesus' name. Remember he said, "If ye shall ask anything in my name I will do it." The only way one can have his sins forgiven is in Jesus' name. You become a believer in Jesus. He says if you will take him at his word, trust yourself to him, he will forgive your wrongs, cleanse you of your sinful nature, and make you a new person.

Now praying in Jesus' name does not simply mean you close the prayer by parroting the words "in Jesus' name."

A woman got sore at the preacher and quit attending services because she said he didn't always close the prayer, "in Jesus' name." Incidentally, isn't it interesting that one quits church because she doesn't like the preacher? That's like a person who quits eating because she doesn't like the doctor.

It is entirely possible to pray in Jesus' name without saying the words. It is even more likely that we say the words without praying in his name. To pray in Jesus' name is to trust him—his power, his person, and his purpose.

Jesus signs the check. The pastor in our story was holding the check in his hand before the eyes of the worried man. The check was made out with the man's name on it. The amount of the check was "All your need." It was signed by Christ Jesus.

"Now," noted the preacher, "there is one more thing— the name of the bank. Where is this account? We are agreed, aren't we, that the Lord has the resources to make the check good?" The man nodded affirmatively. "Let's look again at the passage, 'according to his riches in glory.' It might mean from his glorious resources, but he will understand if we write here the Bank of Heaven, striking through the name of your bank.

"Now does this help you to understand his promise?" The man nodded, "Yes, I think I understand."

"Now suppose," continued the pastor, "you would give me a check for fifty dollars, drawn on the right bank, properly filled out with my name on the face of it and signed by you. Would the check be of any value to me if I simply placed it in my billfold or placed it in the lock box?"

"No, you would have to endorse the check and take it to the bank to get your money."

"Exactly," said the pastor. "We have a tendency to read the precious promises of our Lord and say, 'Isn't that wonderful?' but in practical application, we simply fold up the check and keep God's blessings out of circulation and deprive ourselves as well.

"Some of us place only superstitious value upon the Bible. We keep one in our homes. We wouldn't be without it, but we don't believe it, or we would claim its promises.

"Now, sir, are you willing to take Jesus at his word, trust your whole situation to him—your business deal, your son, yourself, everything; believing you and your son will get the $500,000.00, or something better for you?"

The Bible is true, or it is not true. He will do what he says, or he will not keep his word. Are you willing to go out on a limb?

Will you trust your family need to him, your career, your school need, your marriage, your sin, your everything?

2

People Are Important

People are important. This sounds rather trite, doesn't it? "Trite" is an antonym for freshness and originality. Could it be that trite might be the very obvious thing that I have not done much about?

People are important to business, commerce, and politics. This might be for exploitation. People are important to pastors, evangelists, churches, and denominations. Could this sometimes be for exploitation too?

People do not exist for preachers or church workers, not even for churches. Preachers, churches, and denominations exist for people.

If we had no justification except the first chapter of Genesis, we would know that people are important to God. God created man in his own image. Jesus came to seek and to save people. The despised Samaritans were often the heroes and heroines in some of Jesus' most famous stories. Paul said, in Christ "there is neither Greek nor Jew, circumcision nor uncircumcision, Barbarian, Scythian, bond nor free" (Col. 3:11).

All people are important to God—all kinds of people. Even you are important. Therefore, self-loathing is not a Christian virtue.

One day Jesus was surrounded by some very unchurchly people. He even ate with them, much to the chagrin and vexation of some very churchly people. Jesus often invited himself to associate with such people, as in the case of Zacchaeus and the Samaritan woman. Some of the very churchly people criticized Jesus severely for his association with the unchurchly. Now who were these terrible people with whom Jesus associated, provoking the scathing criticism of the Scribes and Pharisees? The publicans were despised because they were tax collectors and also, perhaps, because they were crooked and corrupt. The "sinners" may have been any persons or groups who did not, or could not, participate in the usual ritual and ceremony of Jewish worship. To the Pharisees and scribes it was bad enough for Jesus to associate with these deplorable people, but for him to eat with them was just too much. Therefore, their muttering and indignant complaining.

The Pharisees represented the "holiest," and the publicans the "unholiest." The scribes represented the "most reputable," and the sinners the "most disreputable." Those who considered themselves holy and reputable complained because Jesus associated with those considered unholy and disreputable. We see Jesus often with these baser groups, which nearly always resulted in criticism. These criticisms, however, often paved the way for some of the clearest teachings which Jesus gives.

In this account (Luke 15), criticism of the religious leaders prompted some of the best-known stories in the New Testament. In answer to these criticisms Jesus told three stories, actually four illustrations, of how important all people are to God.

"Suppose," said Jesus, "one of you has a hundred sheep and loses one of them, do you not leave the ninety-nine in the pasture and go looking for the one lost sheep and keep looking until you find it?" Jesus continues, "When you find it, you are so happy you put it on your shoulders, carry it back home, and call your friends and neighbors together. 'Rejoice with me,' you tell them, 'for I have found my lost sheep.' "

The crowds surrounding Jesus understood exactly what he was talking about. It was shepherd country. They were without benefit of fences, and the sheep must be attended to personally by shepherds and their helpers. To lose one sheep would be to lose much of one's total profit. Therefore, finding the lost sheep was important enough to merit the shepherd's full attention. Sharing the news of the loss would be of interest to his fellow shepherds who had experienced the same thing many times. As a matter of fact, he likely would have inquired of them as he began his search. They would share with him in rejoicing over the sheep when it was found.

Jesus goes on to remind his hearers that since there is so much joy over the finding of one sheep, there is much more joy in heaven over one person who repents of his sins and turns to God for new life. If one sheep is that important to a shepherd, every person is important to God.

Jesus continues with another illustration: Suppose a woman who has ten silver coins loses one of them, what does she do? She lights a lamp, sweeps her house, and looks carefully in every corner until she finds the lost coin. Then she calls in her neighboring friends to rejoice with her because she has found the coin she lost. Even though the coin was worth only a few cents, it was a tenth of all she had. It also might be one of ten coins which married women wore in their hair. If so, it would cause some of the same apprehension as when a modern woman loses a valuable charm out of her bracelet. Anyway, the emphasis is upon a diligent search that would be made by a woman for one lost coin and the rejoicing on her own part and that of her neighbors when the coin is found.

Now, Jesus is saying that if there is that much concern over a lost coin and that much joy over finding the coin, how much more joy there is in the presence of the angels of God over one wicked person who repents. If this coin is so important to this person, how much more important are all people to God?

Jesus then proceeds to tell what has been called by some the best-loved of all short stories in literature. A certain man had two sons, the younger of whom came to his father and asked for his share of the property that he might start out on his own. Most people can easily identify with this story. Either they are young enough to see the son's point of view, or they are old enough to see the parent's point of view. The generation gap is not a new phenomenon. The son reminds the father, perhaps, that this has been discussed several times before but now something must be done. "You don't understand me. I am not like my brother. I have to live my own life and if I blow it, it is *my* life. If I goof it up, it's my business. I don't like the religious and moral restraints. Don't you trust me? Don't you think I have sense enough to live my own life without having somebody point a finger at me all my life?"

Jesus does not say that the father acquiesced because

he thought it was a wise thing to do. Every parent eventually learns that his children must make their own choices. There is a time when decisions must be made for them, but eventually the times come when they have to make their own decisions, even if they are wrong. Of course this is true in our relationship to God. He does not force us to become Christians. He does not force us to live right. He does not make all of our decisions for us. He leaves us free to make our own decisions, even if we make the wrong ones. But even in our wrong decisions, God still loves us.

Jesus uses very few words to make the story move rapidly. Calling in his sons, the father divides the property between them, giving the older son two thirds and the younger son one third. The younger son gathers up his belongings and goes into a distant country where he rapidly throws away his fortune in reckless living. About the time his money and his fair-weather friends are gone, he finds a depression is on. A fellow can't get a job anywhere.

I recall a sermon which I heard when I was about nine years old. The topic was, "The Devil and Tom Walker." Some of the people criticized the preacher for being a little overdramatic and sensational in his sermon on the prodigal son, but at least I have remembered it through these years. The preacher evidently knew about the other short story bearing that title. I found out about that a few years later. However, I have seldom read the fifteenth chapter of Luke without thinking of this country preacher's sermon.

When the young man could not find any other kind of work, he took the most menial job that a Jew could possibly have assigned to him—feeding hogs for a living. As a Tennessee country boy, I could easily picture the fellow sitting on the rail fence watching the hogs eat. He was so hungry that even the hog feed looked good!

The "husks" which the hogs were eating was the fruit of the carob tree. It was a horn-shaped bean, a part of which made fair hog feed but very poor human food. Nevertheless, it made the young man hungry. It was in this state of mind that he began to think of home with the good food, fine fellowship, and even the well-being of the slaves.

The young man comes to himself. Up to now he has been self-centered, immature. A person is never his best self until he is rightly related to God through Jesus Christ. God made us for himself, and we cannot possibly live a balanced, well-rounded life until we are properly related to him. Young people can better make the important decisions concerning career and marriage as they seek the leadership of the Holy Spirit.

Now comes the time for decision. Decision-making is one of the most strategic abilities with which God blesses man. Life is filled with decisions. Over and over we come to the parting of the ways and must decide which direction we will take. Some people never are able to make decisions. It could almost be said that the difference in people is the difference in their ability to make decisions. Some people live out their lives on the basis of other people's decisions. They flow with the current, or are moved by whatever wind that blows. The world is shaped by people of decision (as well as vision). But the young man made a decision and immediately acted upon it. He arose and came to his father, confessing his wrong, perfectly willing to live at home, even in the position of a servant.

This is the point where this story differs from the stories of the lost sheep and the lost coin. A sheep becomes lost just because he is the irresponsible kind of animal that he is. The coin is lost through no fault of its own. These stories illustrate the importance of finding that which is lost. But the story of the lost son illustrates also the necessity for self-discipline. God draws people to him, but he does not force them to follow. The Holy Spirit convinces and convicts of sin but does not force repentance. There is the necessary element of self-recovery.

At this point in the story the curtain rises within sight of the father's home. The father sees the boy as he approaches his home. It is obvious that the father sees him because he has been watching for him all along. Undoubtedly, there had been long, sleepless nights as the father grieved for his wandering son. Always he listened—straining for the sound of a familiar voice. Always he watched —often thinking he had caught sight of the boy—only to discover it was somebody else. Despite his wrongdoing, the son was always important to his father.

On the day of his return the father was watching, ran out to meet his son, embraced him, and kissed him. Immediately he requested that the best robe be brought to replace the rags which the boy wore. A ring and sandals were placed upon him, all indicative of sonship rather than servitude. The father then commanded that the wheat-fattened calf be killed so that they could have a big party celebrating the return of the lost son. This beautiful story with its stirring emotion illustrates the importance of people to God. God despises wickedness, but he loves every wicked person.

The last part of the story especially relates to these Pharisees and scribes with all of their pious religiosity. Jesus describes the older brother who was out in the field dutifully acting like a good son. There is some indication that he was not there because he sincerely loved his father, but because he was doing his duty. He may have been there because he didn't have courage to go anywhere else. Many of those who are most critical of wrongdoing would have done wrong if they had the fortitude or opportunity. Somebody said that conscience gets a lot of credit that ought to be given to cold feet. Well, thank God for cold feet if they keep people from doing wrong.

The older son heard the music and dancing and called some of the hired help to ask what was going on. When he was told, he was so angry that he would not go into the house. He was not glad his brother had come home; he resented the fact that his father had given him a cordial welcome.

The older brother would have enjoyed it if the father had, upon seeing the son, stomped back into the house and said, "I see that scoundrel who called himself our son coming down the road. He will perhaps come back here and ask us to restore him to sonship. We told him before he left that if he threw his life away, he could never set foot in this house again. Let's stick to our guns. Let's make him pay for his wrong doings." Instead, when the father acts like a father, even the Heavenly Father, the older son acts like the weakling that he is.

Because the father loves both of his sons, he comes out and entreats the older brother to come on in and enjoy the party. This father even loves this selfish son who illustrates the religiosity of the Pharisees and scribes as well as some church people of today.

God loves the hypocrites. He loves the people who dutifully go to church every time the doors are open, but in their hearts they are "ravening wolves." There are some church members who quarrel because others do not go to church. Deep down they are glad the other people do not do right—the contrast only makes their "goodness" look better.

I recall a woman who was really revived in a revival. She confessed privately that while she had requested prayer for her lost husband many times, she was now fearful that she had never really prayed for him. She said, "I am afraid I didn't want him to be saved because he might have to give up some of his business practices. If he had to change his business, I might not be able to wear the fur coat and drive the Cadillac automobile to the Woman's Missionary Union of which I am director." She was really revived. Even though these people are apparently more despicable to God, he loves them too. All kinds of people are important to God.

In these emotion-packed stories, Jesus uses many appeals: the pasture, the house, the home, the herdsman, the housewife, the father, the sheep, the treasure, and the sons. Dr. A. T. Robertson closes his discussion on this passage with a message that all of us need to grasp: "Luke was called a painter by the ancients. Certainly he has produced a graphic pen picture of God's love for the lost that justifies forever the coming of Christ to the world to seek and save the lost. It glorifies also soul-saving on the part of his followers who are willing to go with Jesus after the lost in city and country, and in every land and of every race."

3

What God Can Do

One of the best sermons I ever heard was at a Lions Club meeting in a West Texas town. The preacher was a young surgeon. His topic was the ministry of medicine. He began by comparing the ministry of medicine with the ministry of the gospel. He spoke of the relation of both ministries to healing and of the inner relations of these ministries.

The doctor said, "If a patient comes to the doctor, especially the surgeon, scared to death he can't make it, he often doesn't. But, if a patient says to the doctor, 'Don't you worry about me. I am going to be all right. Even if I die, I know where I am going,' that patient usually comes through fine."

The doctor then related the story of a woman who came in for postoperative therapy some weeks after surgery. She said, "Doctor, do you remember me?"

"Of course I remember you. I will never forget you. You were nearer death without dying than any other patient I ever had."

The woman answered, "That's interesting, I never thought I would die. You know, when they rolled me into the operating room on the stretcher, I saw you and Dr. ————. I also saw another doctor. He had a long beard. He told me not to worry—that he was going to pull me through. And Doctor, I was not surprised when I woke up. Neither was I surprised when you came to my room later and told me everything was fine. He had already told me."

The doctor told the Lions Club audience that he was "not going to worry too much about the woman's anthropomorphic concept of God with a long beard. I am just glad she knows the Lord that well."

Do you believe that God can do what only God can do? You may have been in prayer meetings when requests were made for prayer. Someone requested prayer for a child who is to have a tonsillectomy. Someone else requested prayer for a friend who is recovering from a heart attack. Another requested prayer for the bereaved in the loss of a loved one.

Then somebody says, "Pastor, I would like for us to pray for Brother Smith. They have learned that he has a malignancy and can't live. This is a terrible shock for the family, they need our prayers."

'Now the implication is that God can help with some cases, and he cannot help in others. The question then is whether God can do only what doctors and medical science can do. The next implied question is, If God can do only what the doctors can do, can God do anything?

Most Christians believe God uses medical science, but does he limit himself to the resources men have discovered? The Scriptures copiously relate case after case of physical healing. Has God changed his approach or limited his power?

Jesus said, "I tell you the truth: whoever believes in me will do the works I do—yes, he will do even greater ones, for I am going to the Father. And I will do whatever you ask for in my name, so that the Father's glory will be shown through the Son. If you ask me for anything in my name, I will do it" (John 14:12-14, TEV).

What makes us believe what our Lord says about life after death if we do not believe what he says about life before death? If you can trust him to keep his word and to take you to heaven when you die, can you not trust him to keep his word now?

Of course life has a termination point. One day death will come as a result of some condition such as sickness, disease, or accident. But it could be in God's plan to terminate life with some so-called minor illness, or he could will to continue life after some malignancy.

Young People

Can God help young people overcome obstacles as they plan their lives? What can he do for the young man faced with the dilemma of whether to stick to college, do his military hitch, or get a job? What can he do for the girl who is afraid to delay action on a marriage proposal wondering if there will be another chance? What can he do for young people as they try to keep their lives pure, bombarded as they are by nudity, sex, and irreverence? High-pressure brainwashing by the ever-present television set, magazines of many varieties, and the conduct of society in general, all conspire to destroy all restraint. Is there any help from God?

Many young people say with Paul, "I have the strength to face all conditions by the power that Christ gives me" (Phil. 4:13, TEV). Remember, Jesus also said, "If you ask me for anything in my name, I will do it."

The Family

Nearly every daily newspaper has its advice in which column experts answer letters from perplexed wives, bewildered husbands, and mixed-up young people. The popularity of family television serials and "soap operas" indicates that millions of people identify with the roles of the characters.

"I am just living a day at a time. Many days it seems I can't go on any longer," says a twenty-year-old wife and mother.

"I guess I just wasn't ready for marriage," says the husband of one year.

It should also be said that the problem is not solved merely by psychoanalysis. Even when you find out what the weakness is and how you got that way, you still have the problem. Marriage is a knot that cannot really be untied. Even divorce and remarriage does not remove the tangle. The knot can never be completely removed. Is there any help from God?

Parents of young children often feel that if they can ever get their children up to a certain stage, they will have it made. I do not want to disillusion you by saying the worst is yet to come, for there is no "worst" in rearing children. But I do wish to emphasize that there will never be a time as long as you live when you will not need God in behalf of your children. You may be praying for a son in Vietnam or a daughter in some far-away city. Perhaps you are pray-ing for one right in the city with you, but farther away than if he were in Vietnam. In every situation you can be as-sured of the presence and power and love of our Lord.

Can God do anything for you, or will he? Remember what he said: "If you ask me for anything in my name, I will do it." "I have the strength to face all conditions by the power that Christ gives me." Countless parents can re-call those times when they called upon him, and he was a "very present help in trouble." It is exceedingly helpful to review those experiences though time may have dimmed their urgency. Such experiences may even sound childish when you try to share them with others.

A pastor recalled a "simple" experience: One Saturday he told the viewers on his afternoon television service that as soon as he went off the air he was leaving town for some evangelistic engagements and would not return home for two weeks. Leaving the television station, the minister went home to pack for his trip. His wife told him of a rather strange telephone call she had received just after he went off the air a few minutes before. The strange male voice had asked, "Will your husband be preaching in First Church Sunday?" The wife had told him that her husband would not be there and gave him the name of the minister who would be preaching.

The man then asked, "Will your husband be spending the night at home?"

Becoming suspicious, she answered, "He will be home in a few minutes. Would you like to leave your number?"

The next question was still more suspect, "Will he be home, say, at eleven o'clock tonight?"

She answered, "As I said, he is due here any minute. If you will leave your telephone number, I will have him call." With another silly remark, the caller hung up.

Both the pastor and his wife were uneasy about the call when he drove away from home that night. Was it possible that this stranger had heard the preacher say on television he was leaving town? Was he calling just to be sure this was the house where the man was away? About eleven o'clock, as the pastor drove toward his destination, he became very disturbed. He decided to stop at the next public phone booth and call home. Then it occurred to him that fifteen minutes after the call he would still be as uneasy as before. A terrible tragedy could happen in fifteen minutes. Then the answer seemed to come: "If God wants me to be two hundred miles away from home, he can protect my family better than I could if I were home." The pastor then thanked God for protecting and caring for his family.

This simple experience could have been easily forgotten. But soon afterwards, this pastor became an itinerant evangelist, often staying away from home as many as thirty weeks of the year. Many times he thanked God for reminding him of that simple experience and was assured a hundred times that God would meet every need of his family. "But my God shall supply all your need according to his riches in glory by Christ Jesus" (Phil. 4:19).

Physical Needs

Material needs persist in spite of our affluent society. Can God do anything for a man in the throes of financial bewilderment? Will he? "And my God, with all his abundant wealth in Christ Jesus, will supply all your needs" (Phil. 4:19, TEV).

Many a person lives with the threat of failing health. Just as the young surgeon said, those who have the confidence that comes from the consciousness of God's presence usually triumph. It is altogether appropriate for the Christian to pray for the trained minds and skilled hands of those who professionally minister to his needs. It is just as proper to pray for God to go beyond the knowledge and skill of the physicians to bring healing to the body and praise to his own name.

Witnessing

Could it be that one of the real reasons for our failure in helping others to trust Jesus is that we do not really trust him ourselves? When we come to trust his word in our lives, will we be more concerned as we plead with others to trust him for time and eternity?

Faith in God's promises is never more rewarding than in witnessing to others.

During special evangelistic services in a Nashville, Tennessee church, the preacher spoke on the text, "Again I say unto you, that if two of you shall agree on earth as touching any thing that they shall ask, it shall be done for them of my Father which is in heaven" (Matt. 18:19). He sought to assure the people that the Lord not only answers prayer, but he seems to make a special promise to those who cooperate in prayer. Partners in prayer, praying with common compassion and concern, would find their faith strengthened and their needs met.

At the close of the service, a woman went to her Sunday School teacher and asked, "Do you believe what the preacher said tonight about two people praying together with the same concern?"

"Yes," answered her teacher, "Why?"

"Well," the woman said, "that means that if you and I pray together for my husband, he might become a Christian before this revival is over."

The two women went into a Sunday School classroom and prayed together before they left the church that night. They covenanted together to pray continuously for the husband's conversion. The next morning they talked by telephone and prayed. Again that night they met before and after the service in a classroom for prayer. The following night the man professed faith in Jesus as Saviour.

The pastor of the church was so thrilled about this experience that he asked permission to share it with the congregation. Following the pastor's testimony, a man went to his Sunday School teacher and said, "If that woman and her Sunday School teacher could pray and her husband be saved, do you suppose if you and I prayed, my father, who has not attended church in twenty-five years, might be saved?"

The teacher answered, "I would sure be glad to join you in prayer to that end, and I believe God will answer our prayer." They prayed together that night before leaving the service. During the next twenty-four hours the teacher and the man prayed together several times. On the following night the man did not even know his father was present in the service until he came down the aisle, publicly announcing that he too had trusted Jesus as Saviour.

Do you believe that God will hear and answer prayer? God can do what only God can do.

4

Strength for Temptation

The Bible is a book about God and people. Do you know what the first "people story" in the Bible is about? It is about temptation.

I have just looked through my library and files for sermons on temptation. I was surprised to find so few and most of those I found were old. (One exception was Sunday School lesson material. There have been many lessons during the last twenty years on the temptation of Jesus.)

Is there any less need for attention to temptation today? Actually the Bible teaches that the more secure you feel, the greater your danger. "Wherefore let him that thinketh he standeth take heed lest he fall" (1 Cor. 10:12). William James, the noted psychologist, is quoted as saying, "No man has matriculated in the university of life until he has been well-tempted." Is he saying that temptation might be good for you?

Temptation Is Real

The very attributes that make you a human being also

make you subject to temptation. Ambition and appetite may result in worthy achievement. Perverted, these same characteristics lead to pretension, conceit, arrogance, covetousness, intemperance, exploitation, adultery, idolatry, or even murder. The ability to love can deteriorate to the level of lust.

Today's newspaper tells the story of the Federal Grand Jury indictment of a prominent political figure on sixteen counts of conspiracy and fraud. This kind of headline is so common there is a growing tendency to suspect all public officeholders. Some are "as guilty as sin." Some, thank God, prove themselves worthy of their trust. Many whose conduct is unquestionably above reproach face the same temptations as the most guilty. In fact, many of the most guilty were most sure of themselves at the beginning.

"He always seemed like such a nice fellow," the neighbors said of the man who divorced his wife to marry his secretary.

The statement concerning Lot reads so innocently: "And Lot lifted up his eyes, and beheld all the plain of Jordan, that it was well watered every where . . . Then Lot chose him all the plain of Jordan" (Gen. 13:10-11). Sounds like good business judgment doesn't it? He could easily reason that he could take care of himself even though "the men of Sodom were wicked and sinners before the Lord exceedingly" (Gen. 13:13). It was not enough later on, when he had lost his wife and found himself guilty of incest, to say, "the flesh is weak."

An unfaithful husband quoted that passage to the pastor as his only excuse for his sin. He seemed to say it with some degree of boastfulness. He had failed to read the entire verse. Jesus said, "Watch and pray, that ye enter not into temptation: the spirit indeed is willing but the flesh is weak" (Matt. 26:41).

Esau's entire life was wrecked by selling out to satisfy his appetite for one pleasant moment.

Guerrilla Warfare

Temptation does not usually come in the form of one major battle but in many little skirmishes. Most people who read these lines would never knowingly succumb to a terrible temptation. The tempter comes unobtrusively. Resistance wears away. What once appeared sinful looks harmless now. Constant exposure to the television screen makes immorality commonplace. It goes in one eye and out the other. Stealthily, temptation comes in unawares. Alexander Pope describes the process:

> Vice is a monster of so fearful mien,
> As to be hated needs but to be seen,
> Yet seen too oft, familiar with her face,
> We first endure, then pity, then embrace.

The tempter has always practiced the cold war strategy. He gets the victim preoccupied on one front, while he quietly infiltrates the most vulnerable spot. Sometimes Christians become so dedicated to "fighting sin" they become sinners. It is always easier to confess other people's sins.

A woman got up in prayer meeting and confessed that Jesus had given her the victory over drinking, smoking, and dancing. The pastor paid her a visit in a few days to congratulate her. He told her he didn't know she had a drinking problem but was glad that she had overcome it.

The woman responded disgustedly, "I never had a drink of liquor in my life!"

"Well," stammered the flabbergasted pastor as he re-swallowed his Adam's apple and started over, "I am sorry I misunderstood, but you have gotten rid of your cigarette habit?"

"I never had a nasty cigarette in my life," snapped the woman. "What kind of a woman do you think I am?" The pastor didn't dare bring up the other sin she had mentioned and went away feeling the woman hadn't gotten the victory over anything but would likely continue being the same mean gossip she had always been. He now understood that the entire performance had been her way of accusing others while she protected her own ugly spirit and mean attitude. This very attitude may have kept more people out of the kingdom than the sins she "confessed."

The pastor was surprised when a deacon suggested he preach on sin more often. "Were you in church Sunday morning?" he asked the deacon. The answer was affirmative. "What about the Sunday before?" Again he nodded. "What about the Sunday before that?"

The deacon proudly asserted, "I have not missed a Sunday morning, Sunday night, or Wednesday night in seven or eight weeks."

"Well, this surprises me," the pastor said. "I have been preaching a series of messages Sunday mornings on the Sermon on the Mount. I have preached on bad influences, covetousness, judging others, hypocrisy, selfishness, bad attitudes. I thought I had been preaching on sin every service."

"That's not what I am talking about. I'm talking about

preaching against drinking, adultery, gambling and that sort of thing. That's the kind of preaching I like to hear."

"Oh," said the pastor with a smile, "you want me to preach on other people's sins. You know," he continued, "as I looked out over the thirteen hundred people who were present Sunday morning, I don't think I saw over two or three drunks in the crowd. I do not think I saw over six or seven people who had been guilty of adultery the week before, and I don't think gambling is a serious problem in our congregation. But as I looked over the congregation, I think I saw several men who lied for business reasons, several kids who cheated on examinations, several men and women who gossiped about their neighbors, and several parents who criticized the preacher and the church program in the presence of their children. Some cheated on income tax. Some didn't give a full day's work for a full day's pay. I just thought I ought to preach on the sins of which we here in our church are guilty rather than those old mean people over yonder who never will know what I preach anyway."

The devil must smile when religious leaders talk out of both sides of their mouths. You can't ever really trap them. They sneak out by claiming they said one thing when everybody knew another thing was implied. What about the brother who tells you he has recommended you for a position, adding, "You are God's man for the place"? You later learn he has told three or four other fellows the same thing. What about the fellow who recommended a preacher to a church, extolling his virtues, assuring them they would never go wrong in calling him? This "friend" knew all the while the man had made the same errors and shown the same weaknesses in his previous pastorates? He later defended himself by saying that he merely wanted to help a brother in trouble. What about the preacher who introduced each of several different preachers at different times, as "perhaps the greatest preacher in America"?

One can be tempted and fall without ever really knowing that he was tempted. But it is a pattern of dishonesty easily fallen into.

A preacher had gone to a new position. Another preacher warned him about "that music man you inherited. He is poison. You can't trust him. He will stab you in the back." About a year later the preacher and singer were together when they met up with the same "friend." He immediately put his arms around the music man, telling what a wonderful friend he was and added to the preacher, "This is one of the most valuable men you'll ever have on your staff."

Writing of Eve's temptation, F. W. Farrar said, "She dwells jealously on the one thing prohibited, rather than joyously on the many things permitted, until almost unconsciously to herself the tempting voice has passed from the timid suggestion of doubt to the impudent promise of a gain, to the bold assertion of a lie . . . the good that she knows begins to pall upon her, the evil she knows not to shine in alluring colors . . . they who would pluck flowers from the very edge of the precipice must be prepared to fall . . . The lingering thought passes into the vivid imagination, the vivid imagination into the burning wish, the burning wish into the half-formed purpose, the half-formed purpose into the hasty act."

Temptation is not sinful. Nobody was ever tempted more sorely than Jesus. Read the account in the Gospels. He "was in all points tempted like as we are, yet without sin"

(Heb. 4:15). Yielding to temptation is sin. Is there, then, any help from Jesus?

Keep in Shape

Paul writes to the Corinthians and to us, "Every temptation that has come your way is the kind that normally comes to people. For God keeps his promise, and he will not allow you to be tempted beyond your power to resist; but at the time you are tempted he will give you the strength to endure it, and so provide you with a way out" (1 Cor. 10:13, TEV).

In reading the passage it is helpful to go back and read several preceding paragraphs. Begin with chapter 9, verse 24: "Surely you know that in a race all the runners take part in it, but only one of them wins the prize. Run, then, in such a way as to win the prize. Every athlete in training submits to strict discipline; he does so in order to be crowned with a wreath that will not last; but we do it for one that will last for ever. That is why I run straight for the finish line." Then Paul changes the figure to a boxer, "That is why I am like a boxer, who does not waste his punches. I harden my body with blows and bring it under complete control, to keep from being rejected myself after having called others to the contest" (vv. 24-27, TEV). Shadow-boxing is not enough. To prepare for the real fight, there must be real blows. One must learn to protect himself as well as throw the punches.

If a Christian gets too soft, he will be too vulnerable when the inevitable battle with the tempter comes. The Christian keeps in shape by worship, studying God's Word, praying, witnessing, ministering, and by fellowship with other Christians.

Don't Live and Learn

There is a saying that "you live and learn," implying that experience is the only good teacher. Experience is a great teacher but sometimes a hard one. Hard personal experience can often be avoided by taking advantage of the experiences of others.

As Paul goes on in the Corinthian letter: "I want you to remember, brothers, what happened to our ancestors who followed Moses. They were all under the protection of the cloud, and all passed safely through the Red Sea. In the cloud and in the sea they were all baptized, so to speak, as followers of Moses. All ate the same spiritual bread, and all drank the same spiritual drink; for they drank from that spiritual rock that went along with them; and that rock was Christ himself. But even then God was not pleased with most of them, and so their dead bodies were scattered over the desert.

"Now, all these things are examples for us, to warn us not to desire evil things, as they did, nor to worship idols, as some of them did. As the scripture says, 'The people sat down to eat and drink, and got up to dance.' We must not commit sexual immorality, as some of them did—and in one day twenty-three thousand of them fell dead. We must not put the Lord to the test, as some of them did—and they were killed by the snakes. You must not complain as some of them did—and they were destroyed by the Angel of Death.

"All these things happened to them as examples for others, and they were written down as a warning for us" (10: 1-11, TEV).

The sins of the Israelites were inexcusable. These people

had been freed, favored, and fed by a merciful God. But they paid for their sin. "He that soweth iniquity shall reap vanity" (Prov. 22:8). "For they have sown the wind, and they shall reap the whirlwind" (Hos. 8:7).

The Corinthians would be even more responsible for their sin because they had the experience of the Israelites as well as their own. We are more responsible than either, "Do not deceive yourselves: no one makes a fool of God. A man will reap exactly what he plants. If he plants in the field of his natural desires, from it he will gather the harvest of death; if he plants in the field of the Spirit, from the Spirit he will gather the harvest of eternal life" (Gal. 6:7, 8, TEV).

All of this is to say that God keeps us through our temptations as we read his Word and learn of his relations with other people.

Don't Kid Yourself

Don't kid yourself into thinking that you can play with fire without getting burned. Paul continues, "The one who thinks he is standing up better be careful that he does not fall" (1 Cor. 10:12, TEV). It is just another one of the tempter's tricks to make you feel that you are sort of a special person who will not succumb to temptation. Be careful when you are on the edge of the precipice.

Neither can you make the excuse, after you have yielded, that the temptation was peculiar to you. "Every temptation that has come your way is the kind that normally comes to people. For God keeps his promise, and he will not allow you to be tempted beyond your power to resist" (v. 13, TEV).

God Is Real

God never promises there will be no temptations but promises power to resist. Any person is stronger who has resisted the tempter. Abram refused to keep the spoils of war, "lest thou shouldest say, I have made Abram rich."

Job resisted the evil counsel of his wife and others, "In all this did not Job sin with his lips."

Jesus resisted the tempter, or he could never have been our Saviour.

James said, "My brothers! Consider yourselves fortunate when all kinds of trials come your way, for you know that when your faith succeeds in facing such trials, the result is the ability to endure . . . Happy is the man who remains faithful under trials; for when he succeeds in passing that test he will be given life, the prize which God has promised to those who love him" (James 1:2-3,12, TEV).

Peter wrote, "And so the Lord knows how to rescue godly men from their trials."

Several years ago a woman made an appointment with her pastor. When she got to his study at the church she hesitated, saying, "I don't think I should have come. I don't know how to tell you my problem." The pastor waited and with patience and kindness told her that if whatever was troubling her was serious enough for her to worry about, he would be glad to listen. She said, "I don't guess I've done anything so wrong. I'm just afraid I will."

She told about an affair developing at the office where she worked. "This man and I have had no physical relations at all. I know we shouldn't. We are both married, but I'm afraid. The trouble is, I think I want to." Under such circumstances one often finds it difficult to stop even if he knows it is wrong.

After prayer and a better understanding of temptation, she seemed relieved from the fear which could have caused her downfall. She learned how she could face the man with the fact that she was a Christian, embarrassed about the affair. She hoped he could find the same strength in Jesus which she had found.

She never talked with the pastor about the matter again. A few weeks later he knew by her public rededication as well as her changed countenance as she sat in church, that the woman had found the power to say, "Go away, Satan." This has been further verified by the fact that while that pastor has long since left that church, this woman and her husband go to hear him preach if he is anywhere in that part of the state.

You may be facing some temptation. You do not have to face it alone. The dear Lord cares for you and will keep his promise to see you through. He will not force his power on you, but if you will open the door of your heart he will come in. "Listen!" says Jesus, "I stand at the door and knock; if anyone hears my voice and opens the door, I will come into his house and eat with him, and he will eat with me" (Rev. 3:20, TEV).

"I have the strength to face all conditions by the power that Christ gives me. . . . And my God, with all his abundant wealth in Christ Jesus, will supply all your needs" (Phil. 4:13,19, TEV).

Do not worry about tomorrow's temptation. Temptation cannot be met once for all with one big immunization shot. You need the one strong source of cleansing that comes by surrendering your life to Jesus. But you will continue to need him for a lot of "booster shots" along the way.

5

Strength for the Home

Everybody is preaching about the home. Nearly every magazine you pick up has its feature article about the home. The most popular newspaper columns are those written by Ann Landers and her sister, Abigail Van Buren.

A grandmother was asked, "What is the first thing you read after the newspaper comes?"

Grandma answered, "I read Ann Landers before I pick the paper up."

The sharpest advertisers make their appeal to the home, whether they are selling automobiles, boats, cameras or dog food. Speaking of dog food, a grocer was telling how much more dog food he sold than baby food. He quipped, "I don't know whether there are that many more dogs than babies or whether they are feeding babies dog food." Anyway, whoever is selling anything is trying to get his foot inside the door at home.

But do you know who makes more home calls than anybody else? The devil does. He always has. He dared to invade the sanctity of the first home where God himself had performed the ceremony. After that dramatic success the devil returned in the perpetration of fratricide, when Cain killed his brother. Even Noah who had been so blessed of God brought sin into his home with his drunken spectacle. Abram, for fear, lied about his wife in Egypt.

The home of Isaac and Rebecca, begun so beautifully in love, harbored partiality and jealousy and was almost destroyed. The devil came to Joseph, before his marriage, to tempt him through his boss's wife. His refusal to sin cost him a prison term, but God honored his choice by giving him a place of prominence and leadership. The story of Joseph's discipline and temptation is a reminder that a young man's purity is just as important as a young woman's. Christian parents often subconsciously support a double standard.

The devil made evil progress by getting his foot inside the homes of Samson, Eli, Samuel, Solomon, and David when he perhaps could have succeeded in no other way.

Please remember, and never forget, that if the devil dared to invade those homes, he will be showing up at your house.

Why the Home?

Why is the devil so interested in the home? Why does he deliberately concentrate his energies on trying to destroy us by entering the family circle?

One reason is God's interest in the home. It would be difficult to overemphasize the importance of the home to God. This is earth's first institution, and for a long time it was the only social institution. All through the changing centuries, the home has remained the first unit of society. No wonder flowers are used to beautify the wedding environment. For the first wedding God planted and prepared the Garden of Eden.

"And the Lord God said, It is not good that the man should be alone; I will make him an help meet for him" (Gen. 2:18). Jesus, speaking to the subject said, "Have ye not read, that he which made them at the beginning made them male and female, and said, For this cause shall a man leave his father and mother, and shall cleave to his wife: and they twain shall be one flesh? Wherefore they are no more twain, but one flesh. What therefore God hath joined together, let not man put asunder" (Matt. 19:4-6).

The home is so important to God that he builds the strongest fortifications about it. Some of the strongest disciplines in the Old Testament are planned to protect the fidelity of husbands and wives to each other. Of the Ten Commandments, two are directly concerned with the home and three others mention family relationships. In the New Testament Jesus fortifies and intensifies these Old Testament teachings. Paul goes into even greater detail. It is a great testimony to the sanctity of the home when God is called Father, Jesus is the Son, the church is the bride. We are children of God, heirs, brothers and sisters.

God indeed provided for every person to go to heaven every night. So he gave the home, the nearest thing to heaven in this world. The devil, true to his nature, doesn't want anybody to go to heaven any time. He wants everybody to be in hell. Your home will become one or the other.

Emile came home from a date with the fellow she was engaged to marry. She told her mother, "I don't think I can marry Bob. I am so upset I don't know what to do. We are going to break up."

Her mother said, "Oh, it can't be that bad. It's pretty late to break up. You have bought the wedding clothes. Friends have given you showers. The church is spoken for and the minister. You already have the attendants. I am sure you will get it all worked out. Go to bed and you'll see it differently tomorrow."

"But, Mother," she went on, "I have found we differ so much in our religious beliefs."

"But, honey, I thought Bobby was a religious boy. How are you so different?"

"Mother, Bob says he doesn't believe there is a hell. I just can't take that kind of talk."

"Well," smiled the mother, "you go on and marry Bob and we will teach him there is a hell."

Because God desires that every home be heaven, the devil desires that it become hell.

Then there is history's testimony. The decline of nations and civilizations has always been characterized by deterioration of family life. Ancient Rome and Hitler's Germany are vivid illustrations. Modern Russia has seen the handwriting on the wall, and Communist China and Cuba will see it. The devil has exploited fully the changing social scene in America. When America was preeminently rural, strong family ties were necessary to survival. Therefore, a man protected his home—if necessary, with his life.

My father's ancestors were all farm people since they came to this country. Family ties were strong. The children grew up and established their families in the same neighborhood to secure and to be secured by kinsmen. This has all changed. Only one member of the family lives on Sanderson Road, and very few "kinfolks" are left in the community. I never heard of a divorce in my father's family until the present generation. Now the present generation is just as "religious," perhaps more so, than any of which we have records. The difference is that with our rapidly changing society and mores, it is much more difficult to maintain family strength.

Do we toss in the sponge? Is any help available? We will face those questions and find the answers in a few moments. Suffice it to say right now that if the devil couldn't work to destroy your home, there would be no need to have a devil.

If the devil is deprived in his desire to destroy *your* home, he will immediately concentrate his energies and deploy all his forces on the future homes of your children. The kind of home you have is the strongest human force for building or burning your children's homes. If you have a battleground, mentally or physically (especially mentally), you are planting explosives for the homes of the next generation. The psychology of it is indisputable. There is just one way to overcome it. We will get to that later.

The son is never more like his father than when he becomes a husband and father. The fact that he may have deplored and despised his father's habits seems just another contributing factor. The daughter never displays duplicity with her mother more than when she finds herself filling the same role.

Fathers can determine to a great extent the capacity of their daughters to be good wives; mothers have the same unseen influence on their sons. If the father is mean and lacks affection, his daughter may subconsciously fear these qualities in all men and disqualify herself as a good wife. If a mother is domineering or indulgent, the son may never untie himself from her apron strings.

A recent study of the backgrounds of a large group of homosexuals revealed serious maladjustments in all of their homes.

What Can I Do?

Is there any way in the world your home or those of your children can be secured? The devil's success has been so overwhelming, the odds are so fearful—is there any help? Marriage and family counselors and psychiatrists are rendering much help, but most of it at best is like giving insulin to a diabetic. There is no curative value. Is there anywhere we may turn for a preventive answer to this problem?

Do the same thing you do about any other need too big for you to handle. "Believe in and on the Lord Jesus Christ —that is, give yourself up to Him, take yourself out of your own keeping and entrust yourself into His keeping, and you will be saved; [and this applies both to] you and your household as well" (Acts 16:31, The Amplified New Testament). Remember, his salvation applies to the present and future. Turn yourself over to Jesus. "Let go and let God have his way." He can do for you what you cannot do for yourself.

If you surrender completely to him, it will amaze you in the difference you will find in the atmosphere of your home almost immediately. It must, however, begin with you. Don't try to convert other family members until you are converted. Stop preaching and start practicing. Stop prying and start praying.

Use your influence to win your family. It may be difficult, but you are not limited to your own resources. "Trust in the Lord with all thine heart; and lean not unto thine own understanding. In all thy ways acknowledge him, and he shall direct thy paths" (Prov. 3:5-6).

Peter points out that wives can win their husbands, in spite of many handicaps, if they act right (1 Peter 3:1f). This counsel was given to women who, in their society, were virtually nobodies. They were the property of their husbands. Still, Peter insisted that wives could be soul-winners. They often were.

"Try giving yourself away." There is usually no conflict of interest in giving yourself to God and at the same time to your husband or wife. In marriage, two people become one. The husband gives himself to his wife, and the wife gives herself to her husband. Any home can be transformed almost overnight if either mate will dedicate himself or herself to pleasing the other. This applies to every area, whether it is a decision about how to spend your money, how to spend the evening or the most personal and intimate relationships. Isn't it amazing how much time and energy is expended in pleasing other people and how little in pleasing the people who mean more to us than anybody else in the world?

The title of a book caught my attention in the Nashville, Tennessee airport lobby. It was, *A Thousand Ways to Please Your Husband*. It was a cookbook, but even that is not altogether bad.

Your Child Deserves Christian Parents

"Do you know what helped me to become a Christian more than anything else?" This was the question of a man who had been a Christian for several years and was giving his testimony in helping another man. He went on, "A friend told me that if my kids ever had a Christian father, it would have to be me. I got to thinking about it: my children deserve a Christian father as much as anybody's children, and if my children ever have a Christian father it will have to be me. As a result of reflecting upon that, I trusted the Lord as my Saviour."

Other people may be able to give your children some things. In the event of your premature death someone might even help your children with food, clothing, or even education. But nobody else will ever give your child the example of a Christian father or mother. Either you are a Christian, or they will never have that influence. Millions of children will be put to bed tonight who have never had the benefit of a Christian parent's prayer. Every child deserves that right.

Many years ago a young businessman told me, "I have four boys. I am naturally interested in their future. God has given me the ability to make money and naturally I am interested in helping my boys in every way I can in this respect. But I have decided that it might not be best if I give my boys too much too easy. There is one thing, however, of which I am sure—there will never be a time when my boys do not need a father who is close enough to God that he can pray in their behalf."

Does your child, born or unborn, have that kind of parent? Not only is it true that nobody else can give your child a Christian parent, but this blessing is available to you. God has done his part. The provision for your salvation has already been made. The thing left for you to do is to take the Lord at his word. Turn yourself over to him completely to cleanse you and make you a new creature in Christ Jesus. He will help you to find new meaning and power in life not only for yourself but for your family.

6

Personal Strength

He had known success and failure, victory and defeat, happiness and misery, sin and salvation. Now David, the mature, elder statesman reminisces. We like that.

Many of us can recall how we used to hang on to every word from Winston Churchill. Herbert Hoover was perhaps listened to more attentively during his retiring years than ever during his active political life. Regardless of political affiliations, every word from Eisenhower and Truman is carefully read. Magazines clamored for Lyndon Johnson's writings upon his retirement from the presidency. With all of the world censure of Charles DeGaulle, people continued to listen to what he said.

David had reached the December of his life. He had long been king of Israel. Now as an elder statesman looking back, what does David have to say? No, he is not philosophizing about politics and government nor even his own personal successes. As he looks back upon his checkered career—sometimes stormy, sometimes calm; sometimes warlike, sometimes peaceful; sometimes faithful, sometimes disobedient, he reflects upon what God has meant to him through it all.

Looking back through the years of his life, it was easy for David to see that God's hand had been upon him from his boyhood.

During the years I was pastor I found this passage to be the favorite of most people. The first Bible verse that most children ever memorize is, "The Lord is my shepherd; I shall not want." Teenage youngsters see the challenge of the psalm. Parents feel that God can carry them through the heavy burdens of the noonday of their lives. As they face the responsibilities of making a living, making decisions and rearing their children, God is Shepherd. Aged people have always loved the twenty-third Psalm. Shuts-ins request that it be read more than any other passage. Bereaved families often request that Psalm 23 be read at the funeral of their loved ones.

This is a passage which also appeals to Christians and non-Christians alike. Many people have come to trust the Saviour as a result of the message of this psalm. This passage also brings assurance to those who have trusted the Lord as their Saviour.

Turn to Psalm 23 in your Bible. It seems that David makes a statement in the first sentence, and the rest of the psalm is a discussion of his central truth.

God Cares

The word *care* is popular in our day, but we will never understand its meaning until we understand God's loving care. Because of his shepherd experience, David illustrates God's care by showing that God is a Shepherd. This figure is often used in the Bible.

"He shall feed his flock like a shepherd: he shall gather the lambs with his arm, and carry them in his bosom, and shall gently lead those that are with young" (Isa. 40:11). Jesus said, "He calleth his own sheep by name, and leadeth them out. And when he putteth forth his own sheep, he goeth before them, and the sheep follow him: for they know his voice . . . I am the good shepherd: the good shepherd giveth his life for the sheep" (John 10:3-4,11).

"For ye were as sheep going astray; but are now returned unto the Shepherd and Bishop of your souls" (1 Peter 2:25).

"And when the chief Shepherd shall appear, ye shall receive a crown of glory that fadeth not away" (1 Peter 5:4).

"So we thy people and sheep of thy pasture will give thee thanks for ever: we will shew forth thy praise to all generations" (Psalm 79:13).

Now look at David's discussion of what he has said in verse 1: "He maketh me to lie down in green pastures: he leadeth me beside the still waters."

Sheep authorities say if you see sheep lying down on their all-fours resting, they are doing well—putting on flesh. Hungry sheep are restless. This is an exact picture of our world. People everywhere are anxious and restless. They are fearful that they will not be able to make a living, maintain their health, give security to their children, or find any kind of peace of mind.

The masses of people, as Jesus indicated, are like sheep without a shepherd—lost, vulnerable, scared. They are not trusting Jesus. They do not believe that he is the Good Shepherd who will provide and protect. Somebody immediately says, "I know I am a Christian, but I still get worried about things." This is true, of course. Any flock of sheep will sometimes become temporarily disturbed. But it is not long until they are again restored in the confidence that they are safe with the shepherd.

The picture here is that the shepherd will provide the nourishment that satisfies and that he will meet the needs of the sheep of his pasture. He provides water to quench their thirst. These same sheep authorities tell us that sheep do not like to drink from fast-running streams. They prefer still water. The water's edge is also a good place to rest. The psalmist is saying that God provides that which satisfies. God made us for himself and for salvation, and we are thirsty until we find him. The glorious truth conveyed here as elsewhere in the Bible is that he provides for his own.

"He restoreth my soul" (v. 3). Everybody needs restoration. Modern-day living especially uses us up. We run out of fuel and lose our power. We grow weary and discouraged, afraid and nervous, anxious and tense, irritable and unaffectionate. We become cold and callous, dull and dry, sinful and sad. David knew about all of this.

He who had once been so close to God that he was called a man after God's own heart drifted far away amidst the cares and responsibilities of his busy life. During this period, he yielded to a terrible temptation and brought shame and rebuke, embarrassment and sin, to his kingdom, his family, and himself.

Some of the most pathetic passages in the Bible are found in David's description of his sin and the remorse that followed. "My bones waxed old through my roaring all the day long. . . . my moisture is turned into the drought of summer" (Psalm 32:3-4). But he learned about God's restoring love and power: "Blessed is he whose transgression is forgiven, whose sin is covered. Blessed is the man unto whom the Lord imputeth not iniquity, and in whose spirit there is no guile. . . . I acknowledged my sin unto thee, and mine iniquity have I not hid. I said, I will confess my transgressions unto the Lord; and thou forgavest the iniquity of my sin. . . . Thou art my hiding place; thou shalt preserve me from trouble; thou shalt compass me about with songs of deliverance" (vv. 1,2,5, 7).

David goes on to remind us that God leads in the right paths. This also seems to be a figure from the life of the sheep. Anybody who knows about animals knows how they move from one place to another in single file. Go out to any pasture and you will find that animal paths lead in various directions. They go the same way day after day. Every hunter knows that wild animals have the same habits.

I remember driving from Gatlinburg to Knoxville, Tennessee on a beautiful morning. I saw the sun come up over the mountain and flash its rays over the dew of the morning, making every blade of grass look like it was studded with diamonds. I slowed down the automobile to take in the magnificent scene. After slowing down I saw a flock of sheep ambling down the hillside. They evidently had slept in or near a barn at the top of the hill and were moving out into the valley to graze. They were not coming down the mountain, however, scattering in all directions. They were in single file. The leader was in front, and all the other sheep were following one by one.

If I crawled over the fence and took a closer look, I knew I would find that they were following a path. The dew would be beaten from the grass by the first sheep, and because they had likely come down the mountain the same way day after day, the grass would be worn away and a deep path carved into the trail. This not only made it easier for the sheep to follow the path but also made it difficult for them to get out of their rut.

This illustrates our walk with Jesus. He has gone before us. Many others have followed him. They have beaten out a clear path which makes it easier for us to follow. The little chorus which the children sing is true, "Every day with Jesus is sweeter than the day before." But it could also be said that every day with Jesus, it is easier to follow him than the day before. We ought to be better Christians today than yesterday. We can be better Christians tomorrow than we are today. "He leads me in the ruts of righteousness."

David does remind us that all of this which God provides is "for his name's sake" (v. 3). He provides for us because it is in the eternal plan and purpose of God to provide for us. It is for his satisfaction and glory that he provides for us.

The psalmist then goes on to talk about walking through the valley of the shadow of death without fear (v. 4). I am sure he is thinking of the experience of physical death and a great deal more. God has made us with a love and a zest for life. He speaks of salvation as providing eternal life. We are created with a desire to live. By the very nature of the case, we do not like to think of death. But in a real sense death is not death to the child of God. It is true we do not normally look forward to it; we rather fear it and seek by every possible means to delay it. On the other hand when the time comes, he not only gives us strength for the experience but assures us that it is a graduation from a lower to a higher life, a promotion to a richer and fuller life. We dread separation from our loved ones by death, but we do not grieve for them as those who have no hope.

The writer in this passage, however, is including more than the death experience. There are experiences in life which are darker than death for the Christian. They may come in the morning or afternoon of life. These dark and dreadful experiences may come like a tornado that strikes without warning. They may hover at sea for a while like a hurricane as you sit out the fearful hours. In neither instance do you know whether or not you will survive. There are those dark days when you would rather die. You may even wonder how a loving God could allow such dreadful pain.

Those people who have turned to God when the storms of life were raging have found out that he stands by. He will never leave you nor forsake you. In fact, you usually come through the storm a stronger and more mature person.

I once thought Mrs. Cowman, in her devotional book, *Streams in the Desert,* overplayed suffering. I later decided one never really knows Jesus until he is forced to turn to him for help.

Someone has pointed out that where David shepherded his father's sheep, it was necessary for the shepherd to lead his sheep through deep, narrow gorges in going from one green pasture to another. There would be no grass there. It would be dark and forbidding for sheep. Wild animals might hide there to kill or thieves to steal. No sheep could understand the need for being there. However, to give the sheep security, the shepherd would go in front and the shepherd dog would bring up the rear. When they got through, they found sunshine and green pastures on the other side. Many Christians have learned that hardship and suffering often prepares the way for greater spiritual strength and blessings.

"Thou preparest a table before me in the presence of mine enemies" (v. 5). Many times David faced enemies. He had learned that though a host encamped against him, he need not fear. He could enjoy a table spread with food without fear of his enemies.

"Thou anointest my head with oil" (v. 5) might suggest the tender care a shepherd would give his sheep at the end of the day, applying oil where thorns had pricked their flesh. Many different interpretations have been given to these passages. Perhaps all of them are helpful.

God Cares for Me

Not only does God love people, God loves me. Not only does God offer salvation to people, God offers salvation to me. Not only does God answer prayer, God answers *my* prayers. "The Lord is *my* shepherd."

Martin Luther said ours is the religion of the personal pronoun. Notice the personal pronouns in the following words concerning the Messiah: "Surely *he* hath borne *our* griefs, and carried *our* sorrows: yet *we* did esteem *him* stricken, smitten of God, and afflicted. But *he* was wounded for *our* transgressions, *he* was bruised for *our* iniquities: the chastisement of *our* peace was upon *him;* and with *his* stripes *we* are healed. All *we* like sheep have gone astray; *we* have turned every one to his own way; and the Lord hath laid on *him* the iniquity of *us* all" (Isa. 53: 4-6).

Two preachers went on an extended hunting trip into

backwoods mountain country. (I don't know how they arranged it, but I am for it.) They were in a very sparsely populated area. For several days they did not see anybody except each other. Then one day they were surprised to come upon a teen-age boy attending a flock of sheep.

The preachers talked with the boy and were more surprised to learn that he had never been to school. He had never been to town but one time and had never been to church at all. They discovered that he knew almost nothing about God. They wanted to witness to him, but how?

Because he was a shepherd they decided to use, "The Lord is my shepherd; I shall not want." They concentrated on the first five words. They taught him like we sometimes teach small children—on his fingers. The thumb represented "the"; the index finger, "Lord" and so on. Next to the last finger was "my." They especially emphasized this personal relationship, showing how the Lord would be his personal shepherd. They told the boy how Jesus died for him and how he could trust Jesus to cleanse him from sin and keep him in his power. They went their way hoping the Holy Spirit could use their witness.

Many months later the two men were hunting in the same vicinity when they came upon a small house in the mountains which they had missed before. Partly out of curiosity and partly out of a desire to witness again, they decided to knock on the door. At first there was no answer. One of them called, "Hello?" They then heard a woman's voice, "Who's thar?" The preachers explained who they were. The mountain woman opened the door, first just a tiny crack. Then she opened it wide and invited the hunters in.

They sat in front of the open fireplace which on the outside was made of sticks, "chinked" with mud. As the ministers talked with the mountain woman in the meagerly furnished one-room log house, they learned that she lived there alone.

One of the men pointed to a photograph on the mantel above the fireplace, "Who is the boy in the picture?"

"That's my boy," she said quietly.

"It seems I have seen him somewhere," the other preacher commented.

His companion said, "I was just thinking the same thing. Where does the boy live now?"

The expressionless mother gazed into the fire. "He hain't here. He's gone. He had a turrible acci-dent. He's dead."

"I am sorry," the preachers responded in unison.

Responding to their kindly interest she told the story.

"We lived here by ourselves. The boy's pappy left us a long time ago. The boy tended to the sheep. He would go out of a mornin' and come in at night.

"One night the boy told me about seein' some men out thar in the woods. They had told him about God and 'ligion. After that he would sometimes go around countin' on his fingers. He had always been a good boy, always good to his mammy, but he was always a better boy after that." At this point the woman cried briefly.

Then she continued, "One ev'nin' he didn't come in at the usual time. I waited a while and then I commenced callin'. When thar warn't no answer I begin searching for the boy. When dark come on I clam over that mountain yander to the nighest neighbor and them folks jined me in the search. We'uns searched all night. We'uns found a few scattered sheep and knowed somethin' bad had come to my boy.

"About a hour after sun-up the next day, we found his body at the foot of a cliff. I guess he tried to surround the sheep to keep them from cavin' in an' he caved in.

"And you know thar was a curious thing. Maybe you-'uns bein' preachers would understand. When we found the boy's body it looked like he was a-holdin' one of the fingers of his left hand. It was next to his baby finger here." She pointed to the next to the smallest finger. "It looked like he was holding on to that finger with his other hand."

The preachers did understand. This was the finger that represented the word "my." The boy in his dying moments was remembering what the men had told him. As he died to save his sheep, he was trusting the eternal Shepherd who died for him. It is of interest that this is the same finger on which the wedding band is worn. It says, "She is mine and I am hers as long as we both shall live."

The boy had learned that the Lord was his and he was the Lord's as long as the Lord lived. "The Lord is my shepherd, I have had no lack of anything; I have no lack of anything now; I shall not lack anything forever."

Is the Lord your Shepherd? He desires to be. Are you trusting him fully for now and the future?

7

Strength for Witness

Have you ever thought about who might have been voted "Man of the Year" in the early thirties of the first century? One day Jesus announced the "Citizen of the Centuries." He said, "Remember this, John the Baptist is greater than any man who has ever lived." Why do you suppose Jesus rated John the Baptist so high? I believe that John himself answered the question unawares. One day John the Baptist said concerning Jesus, "He must become more important while I become less important."

The all-absorbing objective of John's life was to point other people to Jesus. Wherever we see him he seems to exemplify the knowledge that he was conceived of Zacharias and Elizabeth in their old age that he might be forever pointing other people to Jesus. It was like the old preachers used to say in their prayers, "Lord, help me to hide behind the cross of Jesus." By this they meant that they wanted Jesus to be preeminent. They simply wanted to be a mouthpiece. Now wherever we find John the Baptist, he seems possessed by this obsession.

Read John 1:29. "The next day John saw Jesus coming to him and said: 'Here is the Lamb of God who takes away the sin of the world!' " (TEV).

Now begin at verse 35. "The next day John was there again with two of his disciples, when he saw Jesus walking by. 'Here is the Lamb of God!' he said. The two disciples heard him say this and went with Jesus. Jesus turned, saw them following him, and asked, 'What are you looking for?' They answered, 'Where do you live, Rabbi?' (This word, translated, means 'Teacher.') 'Come and see,' he answered. So they went with him and saw where he lived, and spent the rest of that day with him. (It was about four o'clock in the afternoon.) One of the two who heard John, and went with Jesus, was Andrew, Simon Peter's brother. At once Andrew found his brother Simon and told him, 'We have found the Messiah.' (This word means 'Christ.') Then he brought Simon to Jesus. . . . The next day Jesus decided to go to Galilee. He found Philip and said to him, 'Come with me!' . . . So Philip found Nathanael and told him: 'We have found the one of whom Moses wrote in the book of the Law, and of whom the prophets also wrote. He is Jesus, the son of Joseph, from Nazareth' " (vv. 35-42, 43,45-46, TEV).

In this passage John directs his friends to Jesus. When the friends find Jesus, they repeat the process by bringing still others.

Please note three great things in the story we just read: a great discovery, a great decision, and a great demonstration.

A Great Discovery

First there was a great discovery. These two friends of John discovered that Jesus of Nazareth, thought to be the son of Joseph, is actually the Son of God and the only Saviour of the world. Now I submit to you that this is the greatest discovery that anybody ever makes in a lifetime. Jesus of Nazareth is actually God's Son, the Saviour from sin. He is ready to save anybody any time, if they will turn their lives over to him in faith and trust.

It may be some child who for the first time in his life realizes that he needs a Saviour. He realizes that there is something lacking in his life. He wants to be relieved of his sin, and he finds out that Jesus is ready right now to save him from sin. Or it may be some young person or adult who has been going on in sin for a time. The devil may have a pretty good grip on this life. But the older person learns that Jesus of Nazareth is the Son of God, the Saviour, and he is ready to save from sin right now. I say this is the most important discovery that anybody ever makes in an entire lifetime.

I saw both of these extremes in a single evangelistic service. I was in a revival in a county seat town where the pastor had resigned just before the revival began. They sometimes resign after they have enlisted me to help them in a revival. (Terrible price to pay for a mistake, huh?) I usually resign too when the pastor leaves. In this case, however, the church insisted that I come on because they were sure they would not have a pastor by then. They said they needed revival and that it might help them in getting a pastor. Maybe they thought that if they listened to me preach for a week the people would be glad to have anybody for a pastor! Anyway I went on for the meeting.

I got there on Sunday morning and had the Sunday morning service, then went home with a deacon and his wife for lunch. On Tuesday morning at a Bible study this deacon's wife came to me and said, "Did you notice the woman who was with me in church Monday night?"

I said, "Well, I noticed somebody was with you who was not in your home Sunday. I supposed it was a friend of yours."

She said, "Well, in a way that is true. Did you notice anything different about that woman?"

I was glad she didn't give me time to answer that. I said, "Tell me about your friend."

She said, "I don't want to shock you." She didn't know how difficult that would be. You know, my first job after leaving the farm was in a sheriff's department. After you spend a few months in that kind of environment, you are pretty shock-proof for several years. So, I told her to tell me about her friend.

The deacon's wife continued: "Well, as I said I don't want to shock you, but this woman who was with me last night has, for twenty-five years, operated the most notorious house of prostitution in this state. For twenty-five years I have invited her to church and I have tried to witness to her. For these years she has shopped in our store for herself and her employees. Monday night was the first time she has ever gone to church."

On Monday night I had preached on the subject, "What Kind of Place Is Hell?" I said, "How did she respond to the service Monday night?"

She said, "She sat there and shook all through the service."

"You bring her back tonight," I said. "I am going to preach on 'Forgiveness' " (I just then decided.)

She said, "Well, I think she will come tonight, I have talked with her this morning."

"What did she say this morning?" I asked.

"This woman told me that every time she tried to go to sleep last night, she could see every girl who had ever worked for her calling for help out of hell and she couldn't get to them."

I said, "Well, you bring her here to the service tonight and pray that she will be saved."

The deacon's wife hesitated. "I think she will be in the service, but I am a little scared."

"Scared of what?" I wanted to know.

She said, "I am scared that she might want to join the church."

"Well, praise the Lord! If she is saved, I hope she *will* join the church."

"But you don't understand," the lady said. "If these people here find out who she is, they won't receive her in the church. She is going under an assumed name. Most of them do not know her by sight but they know her name, and if she presents herself for membership, they likely won't receive her."

I said, "Oh, yes they will. You just leave that up to the Lord and the Lord's people. Jesus majored on this kind of thing." I reminded her of the story of the Samaritan woman and the sinning woman and other cases where Jesus demonstrated God's wonderful love and compassion toward all kinds of people.

Tuesday night she was there. When I looked out and saw her in the audience, I could hardly wait for invitation time because I was so confident she was going to trust the Lord. (Did you know services are often shorter if the preacher knows somebody will respond to his invitation?)

I did preach on "Forgiveness" and gave emphasis to

that which is so easy to emphasize from God's Word. God's forgiving love and compassion is always outgoing and overflowing. When I gave the invitation, the woman immediately came down the aisle. As I met her she said, "Will he forgive me?" I assured her, of course, that he would. She trusted the Lord as her Saviour.

Before I leave this part of the story, I want to tell you about the reaction of the people. They not only received her into the fellowship of the church, but some of the women took her in charge and made it a point to pick her up and bring her to services. In many ways they helped her to become oriented to the new life in Christ Jesus.

Now almost simultaneously with that woman's coming down the aisle, there came a woman with her seven-year-old child. Before the service had begun the lady had brought her child back to the pastor's study to talk to me and said, "Last night as you preached, my child decided that she was a sinner and needed to be saved. I have talked with her and prayed with her and showed her what the Bible says about being saved and I think she has trusted the Lord. I just wanted her to talk with you to see what you thought."

Of course I talked with the child and felt that she had fully trusted the Lord as her Saviour. So as the sinning woman was coming down the aisle, here came the woman with her little girl. At the same time that a woman who had wasted her life and contributed to the delinquency of thousands of other lives discovered Jesus, here came a child innocent and pure and unspotted by the sins of the world, acknowledging that she had made the same discovery that Jesus of Nazareth is the Saviour.

A Great Decision

Not only did these friends of John make a great discovery, they made a great decision. They decided to follow Jesus. It is one thing to decide to follow Jesus and another thing to act on the decision. Jesus saw them following. He always does. As a matter of fact, he initiated the idea.

Nobody ever followed Jesus until the Holy Spirit began to pull at his heartstrings. You see, Jesus was seeking you before you ever sought him. He was looking for you before you ever looked for him. He desired that you follow him before you ever desired to follow him. So Jesus turned and saw them following. He said, "What are you looking for?"

Now, this was a little difficult for the men to answer. They had simply been told about Jesus. The prophets had announced the coming Messiah. John the Baptist had made it a little more personal and imminent. On this occasion he had told his disciples, "There is Jesus the Lamb of God." And they started following him. They were not especially prepared to answer any hard questions.

So when Jesus asked, "What are you looking for?" they found it difficult to answer the question. But they came up with a good answer. They replied with another question, "Where do you live?" As if to say, "We don't know just what we are looking for. Our friend has told us about you and that when you came, we ought to follow you. So here you are, and if you will tell us where you live, we will tell you where we want to live. If you will tell us where you are going, we will tell you where we are going."

Jesus did not tell them. He said, "Come and see." This reminds us that Jesus does not outline the entire Christian life for us. He doesn't even tell us all the details of what goes into the saving of a soul, to the creating of a new life in Christ Jesus. He simply asks us to follow him and, when we follow him, he does the rest. So these men decided to follow Jesus.

Sometimes we Christians have a tendency to complicate the matter of being saved. We relate our experiences and some of the outward conditions that surround our experiences. In doing so, sometimes we overshadow the simple trust that is involved in beginning to follow Jesus.

Several years ago I read the life story of Evangelist Sam Jones and some of his famous sermons. In one of these sermons he tells the story of a Methodist bishop preaching in a certain service. Jones himself was a Methodist, and it was natural that he would tell a Methodist story.

The bishop was preaching a profound sermon on conversion. As he preached he got deeper and deeper and the people got sleepier and sleepier; until finally right in the big middle of his message, an elderly man on the front seat jumped up and said, "Brother Bishop, I would like to say a word."

This flustered the bishop a bit. He wasn't accustomed to somebody speaking up during his sermons. When he overcame his fright, he said, "Well, you are a good man. I am sure anything you would have to say would be appropriate. What would you like to say?"

The old man started running down the aisle saying, "I'm going to hell! I'm going to hell! I'm going to hell!" When he reached the back door, he turned and started running back, clapping his hands, saying, "I'm going to heaven!

I'm going to heaven! I'm going to heaven! Praise God, I'm going to heaven!" When he reached the front of the auditorium again, he looked up at the bishop and said, "Brother Bishop, that's what conversion is. I was on my way to hell and I saw my sin and myself, and I turned in faith to Jesus and began to follow him, and now I am going to heaven. That's what conversion is."

Now, the old fellow may have oversimplified the matter a little, just as the bishop may have overcomplicated it. But I wouldn't be surprised if the old fellow was a little nearer right. To become a Christian is to begin to follow Jesus. He does the rest.

Not only is this the way you become a Christian, but this is the way you live the Christian life. The Christian life consists of following Jesus. It has a beginning when we trust him, and he gives us the new life. But it is a daily experience, turning our back on ourselves and our sins in surrender to Jesus. This is what Jesus meant when he said, "Take up your cross daily and follow me." He meant that daily we must let self die, that self be crucified in our surrender to the Jesus life.

Several years ago I awakened early one morning and began to worry about my responsibilities for the day. There were some big decisions that had to be made. I had to counsel some people who had some very serious problems. There were several things in the day's responsibilities that seemed too much for me. I remember I turned on the light, reached over and got an index card off the bed table, and began to write down the things that I had to do. I found myself getting a little nervous about it all. And right in the middle of my anxiety, I recalled a passage of Scripture. It was as clear as could be. Now, the only way you can recall to memory a passage of Scripture is for that Scripture to be in your memory. I recalled the words of Jesus in which he said, "Listen! I stand at the door and knock; if anyone hears my voice and opens the door, I will come into his house and eat with him, and he will eat with me" (Rev. 3:20, TEV).

It seemed clear to me that Jesus was saying, "I know what you have on that card. I know what you face today, and I know it's too many and too much for you. But it isn't too many and too much for me. So I am simply coming by to knock on your door and tell you that if you will open the door and let me come in, I will spend the day with you and you can spend the day with me, and I will help you with these decisions. I will help you in counseling these people, and I will lift these loads which are too heavy for you."

I said, "All right Lord, thank you. I believe you did come by to let me know that you are willing to help me through the day. I am going to remember this, Lord, and if I forget it, I want you to remind me. I will also remind you."

Well, it was a wonderful day. The decisions that had seemed so difficult cleared up. I remember sitting in my study counseling with two people who had very serious problems. I reminded them that there were not three of us in the room but four, and that his presence was much more important than mine. I reminded them they could turn their burdens over to him and he not only would listen with love but that he also would answer with power.

The end of the day came. It had been a wonderful day of accomplishment. You see I had not burned up all of my energy in anxiety and worry and fear. I was so happy about the day that I told my wife about it. As usual she was already ahead of me. She said, "Well, Honey, everyday Jesus comes by and knocks on the door and promises to spend the day with us."

We talked about this for a while. Then we were reminded that he not only comes by every morning and offers to come in and spend the day, but he even comes by every night to give us the necessary rest to prepare for tomorrow. It does take a good deal of stamina to follow Jesus. He desires that we have the necessary rest for it.

A Great Demonstration

Finally, there was a great demonstration. One of the two who heard John speak and followed Jesus was Andrew, Simon Peter's brother. Do you know what he did next? He went and found his brother and said, "We have found the Messiah," and he brought him to Jesus. Now this is the Christian life in action. We read and hear a lot about demonstrations. They may be good or bad. Bringing other people to Jesus is the best way to demonstrate that you have been with Jesus.

You see, the Christian plant, like other plants, normally reproduces itself. The Christian flower, like other flowers, scatters its seeds as it ripens to maturity and life begets life. This is the normal Christian life and anything below this is subnormal. If we are not sharing the good news about Jesus with other people, we are not normal Christians. It is not a matter of knowing how. It is a matter of walking with Jesus and letting the wonderful experiences with him overflow so that they will affect other people's lives. We find somebody who needs Jesus. Immediately, with all the charm and grace of which we are capable, we try to bring him to Jesus. This is soul-winning. This is witnessing. Here we find the necessary strength and guidance and direction for serving the Lord in the most wonderful experience that the Christian can have.

Once during an invitation, a teen-age girl came forward, giving the pastor her hand. He asked her to be seated on the front pew. In a moment I saw she had gone back into the audience again, and I was a little disturbed. I thought, "The poor thing doesn't know she is supposed to stay down here. I hope somebody will go back there and get her and bring her back so she can be here for the preacher to introduce her."

In a moment as I looked down through the crowd, I saw her coming back. But no one had gone back for her; she had gone back for somebody. After trusting Jesus as her Saviour, she had thought about her friend. So she went back into the audience, spoke to her friend, and they came down the aisle holding hands.

I remember an old story from one of our mission fields. In a mission hospital a man had had the cataracts removed from his eyes. A few days after the bandages were removed, the old man was able to see for the first time in many years. Then one day a missionary recognized him coming toward the hospital, holding the end of a rope. On the other end were five blind men. The missionary called to him by name and said, "Where are you going holding that rope with five blind men on the other end?"

The old man answered, "I'm taking my five blind friends to the man who made me see." He was doing what was natural after he had received his sight. The natural thing for us after we have come to possess the new life in Christ Jesus is to share it with other people, to bring them to him. "He must become more important while I become less important."

8

How to Be Sure

"So Jesus went back to Cana of Galilee, where he had turned the water into wine. There was a government official there whose son in Capernaum was sick. When he heard that Jesus had come to Galilee, he went to him and asked him to go to Capernaum and heal his son, who was about to die. Jesus said to him, 'None of you will ever believe unless you see great and wonderful works.' 'Sir,' replied the official, 'come with me before my child dies.' Jesus said to him, 'Go, your son will live!' The man believed Jesus' words and went. On his way home his servants met him with the news, 'Your boy is going to live!' He asked them what time it was when his son got better, and they said, 'It was one o'clock yesterday afternoon when his fever dropped.' The father remembered, then, that it was at that very hour when Jesus had told him, 'Your son will live.' So he and all his family believed" (John 4:46-53, TEV).

Life can be masterful or mad, a muddle or a mess, victory or defeat, success or failure, good or evil. However, it will likely be some mixture of them all. There are none so bad but there is something beautiful, something masterful at least potentially. None are so good but that there is some defeat and failure and evil in their lives. Now why all these variations in our lives? Why are we sometimes up and sometimes down, sometimes off and sometimes on? It is because life is filled with decisions.

Every day we stand at the parting of the ways and decide which direction we will take. Young people stand at the parting of the ways as they decide about a career or life mate. Parents stand at the parting of the ways and decide which direction to take in family matters. In the business world, in the social world, in the educational world—life is filled with decisions. The same is true in our spiritual lives—in our relationships with God and our fellowmen. Which direction shall I take this time? So often it seems that men have a tendency to maximize small things and minimize large things. This is true in some of the most ordinary experiences of life. You read about it in the daily newspapers over and over again.

For example, a man is driving his automobile down the highway. He swerves his car to miss a chicken, crosses the traffic line, and plows into another car. He is killed, and two other people are seriously injured. Now, nobody wants to run down a chicken, but it is a poor sense of values when one risks his own life and that of others to keep from hitting a chicken.

And speaking of chicken, some people would risk a life-size mistake rather than be called "chicken." Did you hear about the chicken that started across the road, saw a car coming and knew he ought to turn around and go back? But he wouldn't do it—he was afraid somebody would call him a teen-ager!

Jesus had something to say about a proper sense of values also: "Will a man gain anything if he wins the whole world but loses his life? Of course not! There is nothing a man can give to regain his life" (Matt. 16:26, TEV). What is the most important decision anybody ever faces? What is the most important decision you face right now?

I recall the story of an elderly preacher who was on his deathbed and invited his children to come and visit him. Among the children who came was a preacher son. One day when the father was feeling pretty well, his preacher son said to him, "You know, Dad, you have been a great preacher. You have meant a lot to many people, and I am sure that there are some things you could say to me that would help me in my ministry. What advice would you give your son who is also a preacher?"

The old man seemed a little embarrassed and said, "Son, when you come as near the end of the way as I have come, you just spend your time thinking about how good God is and how wonderful it is to be a Christian and how soon you are going to be with the Lord always. But," he went on, "Son, if I had any advice to give you and all the other preachers of the land, it would be this: tell the people how to be saved. There are many people who need to be saved, and even those who have been saved rejoice in hearing the story over again. Tell the people how to be saved. Tell the people how to be *sure* they are saved."

Actually when you read in the New Testament about how to be saved, you are also reading how to be sure you are saved.

Our Scripture passage is the story of the Roman official who came to Jesus concerning his sick son. Did you notice the steps followed by the man in coming to Jesus? The same steps which this man followed are the steps necessary for the person coming to Jesus desiring to be cleansed from his sins. Every person who has been saved has consciously or unconsciously followed these steps. If you are not a Christian, you will become a Christian if you will follow these steps.

Now here was a man who had a sick son—so sick that he was at the point of death. The father had heard of Jesus' ministry. A while ago Jesus had performed a miracle in the town of Cana by turning water into wine. Following this, you remember, he had gone to Jerusalem and word had spread concerning his miracle-working power. It was while in Jerusalem that he had the well-known interview with Nicodemus concerning the new birth. Then on his way back up to Galilee, he had the interview with the Samaritan woman who became a Christian and through whose influence a revival was started in Sychar. Now he is back in Galilee again.

The man who lived at Capernaum, some twenty-odd miles away, heard of Jesus' return and decided to go over and see him in behalf of his sick son. Now you can easily see that the man followed at least three steps in coming to Jesus. For one thing, this man knew that he needed Jesus' help. In the second place, he came to Jesus and asked for help. And in the third place, he took Jesus at his word. Now, these are the three steps that are necessary to a person's becoming a Christian.

He Knew He Needed Jesus

This man knew that he needed the help of Jesus. Nobody had to tell him. Very likely, he had gone to the best physicians he could find in his community, and they had shaken their heads negatively. There was no more they could do for the son. So he came to Jesus and said, "Come and help my son or he will die." There was no lack of sincerity in this man's coming to Jesus.

If you have been a parent very long, very likely there has already been a time when you knew that you needed the help of Jesus more than anything else in behalf of your child or some member of your family. If that time has not already come, it very probably will come.

I remember sitting in my study on a Saturday afternoon talking with the Sunday School superintendent of the church where I was pastor. The telephone kept ringing, and I kept answering it. Finally the superintendent said to me, "Pastor, if you keep on answering that phone, we won't be able to have our conference. All of these people are calling to find out when their children are going to be returning to town, and we don't know any more about it than they do. You have a private phone where anybody can call you if they have to have you, so I wouldn't answer that other phone every time it rings."

Well, the truth of the matter was that it kept ringing constantly. A group of our young people had gone to another city to be in a music clinic and they were due to return that afternoon. But about the time the superintendent finished with his suggestion, the phone rang again, and I almost automatically answered it. Immediately, I heard the crying voice of a girl on the other end of the line as

she said, "Pastor, we have had a terrible automobile accident, and your daughter has been seriously hurt. Will
you go to Memorial Hospital as soon as you can?"

Of course I rushed to the hospital. The superintendent
went to try to find my wife who could not be reached by
phone at the moment. I got to the hospital before they
brought my daughter in and waited in the emergency
room. Soon they were bringing someone in on a stretcher.
Someone asked, "Is that your daughter?"

The injury was so serious that I didn't recognize her,
and I said, "No, that isn't my daughter." But she recognized my voice and called, "Daddy." My wife soon arrived. As we stood in the emergency room for the preliminary examination and treatment, I remembered this man
who came to Jesus requesting that Jesus come over and
help him, or his son would die. I tried to pray the same
kind of prayer. I am thankful to say that God heard and
answered the prayer. Though the damage was serious in
the area of her face and head, if she were to walk in the
room where you are now sitting, you likely would not recognize she had ever been in such an accident.

Of course, I would like to say, parenthetically, that
sometimes the Lord does not answer prayer by saving our
loved ones from catastrophe. Sometimes he does other
things for the individuals concerned. But I am illustrating
the man's recognition of his need for Jesus.

Now, I say to you that if you know you need Jesus in
the forgiveness of your sins, Jesus is available. If you say
to me, "I have no need of Jesus. I can take care of my
life myself," I regret to say to you that for you, no salvation is available. If you say, "I have sinned and need
Jesus," I am happy to say you have already taken the

first step toward salvation. But you must know that you need Jesus' help.

Now it requires no stretch of the imagination to know that you need Jesus' help. Everywhere you look in the Bible, you will find a reminder of your sin and delinquency. Throughout the Old and New Testament, this theme is central. We are also reminded that the price of sin is death.

This fact was made known in the very beginning when God told our first parents that eating the forbidden fruit carried the penalty of death. Ezekiel later reminded us: "The soul that sinneth, it shall die" (18:4). Paul said, "The wages of sin is death" (Rom. 6:28). So here we stand, knowing that we have sinned and recognizing that the price for sin is death. We remember that Jesus came into the world and died for our sins. It is easy to see that we need his help. And I am happy to say to you that if you recognize your sin and need for Jesus, the first step in your soul's salvation has already been taken.

He Asked Jesus for Help

Not only did this man know that he needed Jesus' help, the man came to Jesus and asked for help. Now that is a reasonable thing to do, isn't it? You act on that principle every day in business, in politics, in romance, in every area of your life. There is something that you need or desire, and you go after that something. You must act upon the same principle in the matter of finding certainty and assurance concerning your own relationship with Jesus. So you come to Jesus and ask him for help.

This man was completely sincere in coming to Jesus. The twenty miles that he had to travel, perhaps by foot, was no serious problem. Who would not walk twenty miles in behalf of a dying child? But who would not also seek earnestly for forgiveness of sin and eternal life by the power of Jesus Christ? This man came to Jesus and asked for help, and he made the request very simply. In other words, he prayed to Jesus. He said, "Sir, come with me before my child dies."

Now there was one weakness in his prayer, and Jesus knew this beforehand. Jesus said to him, "None of you will ever believe unless you see great and wonderful works." The people were accustomed to miracles being performed with a great deal of sensation, a great deal of fanfare. The man just knew that Jesus would have to go with him from Cana to Capernaum, stand by the bedside of his son, perhaps anoint him with oil, and otherwise go through the usual performance of healing. He was perfectly sincere in his prayer, but the one mistake he made was in trying to tell Jesus how to answer his prayer.

Do you know that there are people all about us who know they need to be Christians and trust Jesus as Saviour? They plan sometime to accept him as Saviour, but they have not done so yet, because they are trying to tell the Lord how to save them. They have heard people say that it happens in a certain way, and they are expecting it to happen in that certain way. One person says, "I plan to be a Christian and if it ever hits me, I will ask the Lord to save me." Now, if *what* ever hits you? Where in the Bible are we told that something hits you and you become a Christian?

Somebody else says, "I'll be a Christian someday, but I'm afraid just now that I'm not ready. I'm just afraid that I can't live up to it—that I can't hold out." But where in the Bible does it say that a person must come to the place where he can "live up to it" or "hold out" before he becomes a Christian?

Somebody else says, "I will be saved if I ever have that feeling." But what "feeling" does the Bible say that you must have to become a Christian?

You see, the only information we have concerning becoming a Christian is the information we get from the Bible or from the experiences of other people. I would rather trust what the Bible has to say about it, wouldn't you? Well, what do you have to do to become a Christian? We read in the New Testament a very interesting story about a man who came to two other men and asked them what he must do to be saved.

Nearly everybody is familiar with the story of the jailer who came to Paul and Silas and asked for help. Let's look at his question and the answer of these men. The jailer asked, "What must I do, sirs, to be saved?" (Acts 16:30, TEV). Now what was their answer? Did they say, "If it ever hits you, you'll know it"? Did they say, "If you'll join the church and be baptized and go through the usual public performances and ceremonies, you will be saved"?

This man asked, "What must I do, sirs, to be saved?" And Paul and Silas answered: "Believe in the Lord Jesus, and you will be saved—you and your family" (v.31, TEV). This is what you have to do to be saved. Don't try to tell the Lord how to save you. Let him tell you. He is the one who does the saving. When you go to the doctor, you do not tell him what the prescription is to be. He prescribes the treatment or performs the operation. Now Jesus is the one who performs the salvation operation. He has full knowledge about salvation, and he is the one who must do it. So, why not just let Jesus do it in his own way? Don't try to tell him how.

He Believed Jesus

And then came the third step. Jesus said to the man, "Your son will live." The man believed Jesus' words and went home. Now right there is where a soul is saved. At the very moment you take Jesus at his word, you can be confident that your life is in safe hands, that your salvation is assured. When the man believed the words of Jesus, he went.

The Scriptures tell us that on his way home, his servants met him and told him the good news, "Your boy is going to live." He asked them what time it was that his son got better. He already knew what the answer was.

They said, "It was one o'clock yesterday afternoon when his fever dropped." The man remembered that it was at the very hour when Jesus had told him, "Your son will live."

Now, the very moment you take Jesus at his word and turn your life over to him in complete surrender, that very moment you can be sure you are a child of God, that your name has been written indelibly in the Book of Life. You don't have to understand all the complicated, theological questions that will come to your mind concerning salvation. It is not necessary for you to memorize large portions of Scripture or commit to memory certain sets of theological beliefs.

When I became a Christian I did not know very much

about it. As a matter of fact, the average seven- or eight-year-old child who has been reared in a Christian home and has been in Sunday School regularly, knows more about how to be saved than I did when I became a Christian. I did know that I needed to be saved. I had known it for some time. I had been trying to work my salvation out for two years, and I was about to give up in desperation. I was not in a church service that day. I had been in church services all my life. I had heard my father and mother and Sunday School teachers tell about their Christian experience, but it had been very difficult for me to apply it in my own case.

On this particular day while I was alone in a field, I got to thinking about it and I said to myself, "If I were to die, I would go to hell." Now some folks say that children never think about hell and that it ought not to be mentioned to them. But I know I thought about it, and I didn't want to go there. So, I got down under some bushes on my knees (it was not necessary to get on my knees, but I did). I got on my knees, and I remember praying something like: "Lord, if I were to die, I'd go to hell and I don't want to go to hell. I want to go to heaven. I want to be a Christian while I live, but I don't know how."

I remembered they had told me that if I would call on Jesus he would save me. So I said, "Lord, I am asking you to save me from my sins right now." Then I thanked him for saving me and went on my way.

I suppose if I had met somebody out there in the field that day and he had asked me if I were a Christian, I would have said, "Yes." If he had asked me how I knew, about all I could have said was that Jesus said he would save me if I would believe in him and call upon him. I believed in him and I called on him; therefore, he saved me. This is the one requirement. If you have never done so up to now, if you will call on Jesus in faith right now, he will save you right now.

9

How to Be Happy

Are you happy? I did not ask if you have no problems or troubles of any kind, but are you happy? I did not ask if you deserve happiness. I am asking if, in spite of these handicaps, you are happy.

Jesus means for his people to be happy. Listen to what he says:

" 'Happy are those who know they are spiritually poor: the Kingdom of heaven belongs to them! Happy are those who mourn: God will comfort them! Happy are the meek: they will receive what God has promised! Happy are those whose greatest desire is to do what God requires: God will show mercy to them! Happy are the pure in heart: they will see God! Happy are those who suffer persecution because they do what God requires: the Kingdom of heaven belongs to them! Happy are you when men insult you and mistreat you and tell all kinds of evil lies against you because you are my followers' " (Matt. 5: 3-11, TEV).

In a study of the First Epistle of Peter, I discovered

an emphasis on happiness, holiness, and humility. The
present discussion has to do with happiness. I am not dis-
counting the other teachings in the epistle. Neither do I
think I am doing violence to the book in pointing out the
happiness element. I suggest that you keep your New
Testament open to "The First Letter from Peter," the
Good News for Modern Man translation, if possible.

A few years ago I was preaching in a county-wide tent
revival. One of the preachers on the steering committee
was a miserable man. People were afraid to ask how he
was feeling. He would tell them. Everything was bad: his
church, his wife, his children, his health, everything. Such
a state of depression is bad for anybody, but for a spiritual
leader, it is a thousand times worse.

I saw a miracle. In less than two weeks, this man's entire personality changed. He became vibrant, positive,
cheerful, and enthusiastic. He came alive. As a matter of
fact, during this period somebody started a rumor that
could have broken him, but instead, it seemed to strengthen
him. What happened to the man that changed his entire
life? He came to a new understanding of what the Christian
life really is.

What is there to be happy about in a world filled with
sadness, sorrow, sin, and disappointment?

You Are Elected

Election day is a glad day for those who are elected.
An acquaintance of mine was always running for political
office and always getting beaten. One time he was almost
elected, but the vote count was not quite enough. He became so despondent that his wife and friends became
concerned. They feared a breakdown.

One day his wife found him in the living room reading the Bible. She wisely went on into the kitchen without saying anything to him. A few minutes later he rushed into the kitchen with a big smile and said, "Honey, I've been elected."

His wife thought, "Oh my, it has happened!"

He was insistent. He was holding his Bible in his hand. "I've been elected. I've been elected." He pointed to the words, "Elect according to the foreknowledge of God" (1 Peter 1:2). "Even though I was not elected by the people, God has elected me to a much higher office. Isn't that far more important?"

The verse reads, "You were chosen as a result of God the Father's own purpose, to be made a holy people by his Spirit, and to obey Jesus Christ and be made clean by his blood" (TEV). The Father, the Spirit, and the Son all participated. Isn't that something to be happy about?

You Have New Life

There is magic in the word "life." Life is everything. Everybody everywhere agrees. The Bible agrees. God created life. Jesus came that we might have life. He gives eternal life.

Has life become drab, dull, even dead? "Let us give thanks to the God and Father of our Lord Jesus Christ! Because of his great mercy, he gave us new life by raising Jesus Christ from the dead. This fills us with a living hope" (v.3).

You see it is not necessary to be drab, dull, dead. You can have new life. It is not a matter of being religious or good. It is a matter of being *alive*. Jesus one day talked to a very good man who was very religious and well respected, but he was dead. Jesus said to him, "I tell you the truth: no one can see the Kingdom of God unless he is born again." Paul said in a letter to friends of his day and ours, "In the past you were spiritually dead because of your disobedience and sins."

If you are a Christian, you have been chosen and destined by God the Father, sanctified by the Spirit, and made clean by the blood of Jesus.

Don't be afraid of that word "blood." It is there. Why? The price for sin and disobedience is death. This is the law of God, unchanging and irrevocable. Jesus paid the price by dying on the cross, sacrificing his own blood. By his death we are made alive, if we believe in him.

A great and well-known preacher recently was quoted as criticizing the *Good News for Modern Man* translation of the New Testament because the word "blood" is not used. He had not read far enough. It is also ridiculous for religious leaders to criticize the use of the term when it is there.

The glorious good news is that Christ died for our sins, he was raised from the dead and offers new life to all who will call on him in faith.

Do you have the new life? God offers it! Do you have the new life? Then give thanks to God and be glad. You will be happier every day you practice the new life.

You Have an Inheritance

Have you ever received an inheritance? Do you expect to? I recall a family in other years that unwisely waited for an inheritance. They were so sure they would receive a sizable inheritance that they lost their incentive to work and produce. When they needed money, they mortgaged their present property and waited for the inheritance. During the depression of the twenties and thirties, they spent everything. The big problem was that, during the same depression, those from whom they expected an inheritance lost everything too.

If you are a Christian you have an inheritance being kept for you. You have been born to an imperishable inheritance. "So we look forward to possess the rich blessings that God keeps for his people. He keeps them for you in heaven, where they cannot decay or spoil or fade away" (v. 4).

There is a bank that will never fail. There is an impregnable safety deposit box. Nobody can get to it to tamper with it, wrongly invest it, nor steal from it; not even the devil. It will be in heaven when you get there. You can enjoy life in this world, and one of its joys is what you look forward to in heaven. Be happy!

You have perhaps also known some people who would have received a nice inheritance, but they did not live long enough. In the case of the heavenly inheritance, this cannot happen. The inheritance is kept safely for you, and you are kept for the inheritance.

"They are for you, who through faith are kept safe by God's power, as you wait for the salvation which is ready to be revealed at the end of time" (v. 5). Your inheritance cannot be destroyed; neither can you. You are garrisoned under the protection of his power.

It is so easy to limit one's life to what the eyes can see and the hands can hold. Over against these things which slip through our fingers while we hold them—these clothes that fade out while we wear them, these properties that diminish while we possess them, these bodies that deteriorate while we feed them, these friends who fail us while we trust them—he assures us of life imperishable that does not fade away.

We listen with trembling heart as the scientist tells us how quickly this very planet may explode. By our very nature we pray it will not be so, but even if it is, this new life in Christ, this inheritance cannot be taken away.

No wonder Peter adds, by divine inspiration, "Be glad about this, even though it may now be necessary for you to be sad for a while because of the many kinds of trials you suffer" (v. 6).

You May Suffer

You may say, "I can see how Peter could admonish people to be happy back there in Bible times when everything was beautiful and uncomplicated. But it has no relevance to us now with our social complexities, our senseless wars and violence. Nothing is certain now."

A casual glance at history will reveal that those people who first read this letter were to suffer some of the most atrocious persecution in human experience. Some would be crucified; some would see their loved ones slain and their bodies mutilated. Some would have their live bodies wrapped in the fresh skins of animals for other animals to attack. This was the price they had to pay for even claiming Christ as Lord. We talk about untrustworthy government officials. They could trust their political leaders—to destroy them!

Why do good people have to suffer? "Their purpose is to prove that your faith is genuine" (v. 7). It would be an oversimplification to sum up all human suffering in these words, but this much is true.

No normal person desires suffering, but in Christ, people are stronger following suffering. Not more than five days ago I heard two men talking about a mutual friend. Said one, "This man's life seems to deepen and his leadership grow stronger as he gets older."

The other friend said, "This has been especially true since he had that tragic accident when his body was broken to bits and he thought he would die."

"Even gold, which can be destroyed, is tested by fire; and so your faith, which is much more precious than gold, must also be tested, that it may endure. Then you will receive praise and glory and honor on the Day when Jesus Christ is revealed" (v. 7).

The follower of Jesus is not promised a life free of suffering. He is assured of happiness even while he suffers.

You Are Better Off than the Prophets

The Old Testament prophets talked about the blessings which would come. We, in our day, have seen what they talked about.

"It was about this salvation that the prophets made careful search and investigation; they were the ones who prophesied the blessings that God would give you. They tried to find out when the time would be and how it would come; for the Spirit of Christ in them pointed to this time in predicting the sufferings that Christ would have to endure, and the glory that would follow. God revealed to these prophets that their work was not for their own benefit, but for yours, as they spoke about the truths which you have now heard" (vv. 10-12).

What have we to be happy about? Every good thing the prophets talked about.

The Angels Don't Understand

As a Christian, you are much better off than angels. They cannot even understand what you enjoy. "The messengers of the Good News, who spoke by the power of the Holy Spirit sent from heaven, told you these truths. These are truths which even the angels would like to understand" (v. 12).

There is nothing superficial or shallow about the New Testament concept of happiness. It is not an opiate for little people. Christianity is not a fairy tale. Happiness is not make-believe. It is not merely positive thinking. It is realistic—hard as nails.

Christianity is not a religion of "pie in the sky, when you die, by and by." The real truth is that man is made for more than this earth can offer. Therefore, he is not limited to the earth. By the power of Christ he comes to understand unrealized ambitions. One day his dreams will come true. Man was never meant to be fully satisfied with physical existence, because he is more than physical.

Those things that men's minds now only get a glimpse of will one day be seen and comprehended. Man's loftiest moments *now* will not even be up to norm *then*. We get a tiny taste *now*. We will fully enjoy *then*.

"You love him, although you have not seen him; you believe in him, although you do not now see him; and so you rejoice with a great and glorious joy, which words cannot express, because you are obtaining the purpose of your faith, the salvation of your souls" (vv. 8-9).

10

How to Be Holy

Holiness and hypocrisy are often confused in language as they are in fact. People tend to shy away from using the words "holy" and "holiness" for fear they will be misunderstood. A worse tendency is to shy away from the practice of holiness for fear of being misunderstood.

A few years ago three speakers representing three Baptist groups in the United States were speaking in Canada to an evangelism conference. One of the visitors asked another, "Don't these Canadian Baptists tend a little toward holiness?" The answer was, "I've never known Baptists to be too holy."

Again we go to "The First Letter from Peter." We will observe some admonition to holy living and then some of the reasons why. Again I remind you that the purpose is not a complete exposition or exegesis of the Bible material. Neither is this an exhaustive study of holiness. Rather, we are looking at holy living as it is discussed in the passages comprising our study (1 Peter 1:13-2:17). There is some overlapping in our discussion of happiness, holiness, and humility. Obviously, Peter did not use our outline. I do not expect anybody else to do so necessarily. I repeat that we are looking at happiness, holiness, and humility as seen in these passages. Our objective is the improvement of our lives as we gain strength for living.

Get Out of the Briar Patch

The dress of Peter's day was different from ours today (although we are moving in their direction). They wore long robes which created some difficulty in active physical exercise. It would be very easy to get one's robe tangled in bushes and briars on the side of the road or path. To overcome this handicap, the people of that day wore girdles which held the other clothing in place. To "gird up the loins of your mind" is to keep spiritually alert and avoid the distractions.

If you think living the Christ-life is easy, you probably aren't living it. You are tangled up in the bushes and don't know it. You see, you can get tangled up on the way to church, or even while you are there. A lot of mean things are thought, said, and done by people who are in church every time the doors are opened. Attending services is not an end in itself. While church work is not sinful, neither is it an immunization from sin. While church work is a part of holy living, it was never meant as an escape mechanism. People whose hearts are right will be active in the church. The reverse is not always true.

If church people can get tangled up in the briars, think how much more likely it is for those who are not church people. If you excuse your non-Christian life by pointing to the weaknesses of the church and church people, you didn't even get as far along as they. No, they are not meaner than you. You are meaner than they.

While some people die in the hospital, they usually do not die because they are there. Some nonsmokers have lung cancer, but it is not caused by nonsmoking.

"Have your minds ready for action, then. Keep alert, and set your hope completely on the blessing which will be given you when Jesus Christ is revealed" (1 Peter 1:13, TEV).

Be a Nonconformist

Not only are Christians to avoid being like other people; they are to avoid being like they themselves used to be. All too often people "make a profession of faith," and it makes no more difference in their lives than joining the Garden Club or becoming a member of the Chamber of Commerce.

To become a Christian is to become a new creation. To be born again is to begin a new life. Old things are passed away and all things become new. It is not "something old and something new." Everything is new.

The late Dr. John R. Sampey is often quoted in his admonition to students: "Give the keys to all the rooms of your life to the Lord." We tend to compartmentalize our lives. We have separate compartments for business, family, recreation, education and religion. It is rather easy to keep the living room presentable for our Lord. But unless he has access to bedrooms, kitchen, dining room, family room, attics, closets and garage, he will not live in the living room. "Instead, be holy in all that you do, just as God who called you is holy" (v. 15).

You cannot keep the bugs out of the living room by spraying only that room. A "Sunday suit" is not enough. Jesus wants the entire wardrobe.

When one becomes a Christian he does not "act different"; he *is* different. "Do not allow your lives to be shaped by those desires that you had when you were still ignorant" (v. 14).

Be Afraid

If you are afraid of sin, you don't have to be afraid of anything else. We live in an environment of sin. We are caught up in it unawares.

Here is a man who has spent his life as a Christian leader. God has used him in changing other lives. His influence reaches out. People are attracted to him, and he points them to Jesus. He speaks and writes to the glory of God. One day in a moment of weakness—maybe physical fatigue, maybe self-trust and overconfidence—he leaves his armor off. He is gradually led into sin. His entire life and influence are ruined.

Your case may be less dramatic, and you are still unaware of your sin. You have developed an ugly attitude, a mean spirit, or impatience with others. It is necessary to be constantly on guard. The best way is to "keep your eyes on Jesus."

"You call him Father, when you pray to God, who judges all men alike, according to what each one has done; you must, therefore, spend the rest of your lives here on earth in reverence for him" (v. 17).

Love One Another

A man said half-jokingly, "I can always recognize the members of ———— Church in a restaurant even if I don't know them. Do you know how I recognize them? They are always criticizing the preacher or some other members of the church."

"Unlove" is detestable and despicable anywhere, but among members of the fellowship of saints, it is most deplorable.

Criticizing others grows out of a sense of inferiority, guilt, and insecurity. When you develop a Christ-love for others, you begin to grow personally. You become mature enough that you do not feel the necessity of lifting yourself by your own bootstraps. Therefore, no more need to reduce others to your size. The only way to practice Christ-love is to be possessed by him.

"Now that you have purified yourselves by obeying the truth, and have a sincere love for your fellow believers, love one another earnestly with all your hearts" (v. 22).

Grow Up

Being grown-up requires that you first be a baby. Babies are possessed by desires, which when fulfilled, help them to grow up. One of these desires is hunger. Babies are always hungry. They just can't seem to get enough milk. They drink until they hurt; then they drink some more to be sure. Babies literally drink until it overflows, to the chagrin of those who hold them.

What does a baby's gluttony have to do with the Christ-life? Just as the normal baby is always thirsty for milk, the normal Christian is to be always thirsty for pure unadulterated spiritual food. Do you love to read God's Word? That is normal for you as a Christian. When you come to the place you do not love it, you need a checkup. Your growth will be stunted.

One of the best proven ways of getting to a person's purse strings is to get to his heartstrings with the picture of an emaciated child. Our hearts almost break when we see a child not developing mentally or physically. What a shame we cannot see ourselves inside and out.

What are the first signs of spiritual retardation? Malice, deceit, pretense, jealousy, envy, slander, recrimination. To display these symptoms is to reveal a sad state of health.

"Rid yourselves, therefore, of all evil; no more lying, or hypocrisy, or jealousy, or insulting language! Be like new-born babies, always thirsty for the pure spiritual milk, so that by drinking it you may grow up and be saved" (2:1, 2).

To be born is one thing. To have good health is another thing. To be born again is to begin the new life. You come to Jesus for the new birth. You come to Jesus for continual growth.

Keep Your Eyes on the Homeland

A few years ago it was my privilege, along with two other Americans, to join missionaries and preachers from all over the Orient for an evangelistic crusade in Taiwan. Our first week was in the Taipei area and the second in Tainan.

Our opening service in Tainan was on Mother's Day. I was very surprised to have an attractive lady approach me with two rose buds, a red one and a white one. "Which do you wear?" she asked through an interpreter.

It had never occurred to me that they observed Mother's Day there. I had begun the day thinking of my mother and my children's mother. I was happy I could still wear a red rose.

When we got into the worship service, I saw that red

roses were predominant all over the audience. I remarked to Miss Pearl Johnson, our missionary, "Isn't it wonderful that all these people still have their mothers?"

"They hope their mothers are still living," said Miss Johnson. "Most of them have not seen their mothers for more than ten years. They were left on the mainland of China."

This was just another reminder of what I had already learned. Here was a group of transplanted people with their eyes still on the homeland. They expect to go back. They believe the Bamboo Curtain will be pushed back, and they will recover their homeland from the Communists. However thankful they are for their freedom, you always have the feeling they are thinking and planning toward the day when they will go home.

Peter was addressing himself to dispersed people; strangers, pilgrims, and sojourners. They tell us that as the Hebrews were taken captive to other lands, they always built their synagogues so that they were facing Jerusalem.

We are reminded that this world is not our permanent home. We live here only temporarily. We do well to keep our eyes on the homeland, never allowing immediate surroundings and circumstances to pervert our lives. We are to be careful never to embarrass the kingdom or King of our homeland.

You Are a Child of Obedience

What higher motivation could one have for holy living than that he is a son of God? We are children of obedience just as we were once children of wrath. We are children of a holy Father. We were begotten to holiness.

A young son was taking his first plane ride alone to be

with his evangelist father in another city. He seemed a little nervous as the plane's departure was announced. "Are you scared?" asked his mother.

"I'm not going to think about being scared," he said. "I'm just going to think about seeing my father when I get there."

The Christian will not allow unpleasant circumstances, fear, or temptation to keep him from honoring his sonship. We are sons of a holy God who has called us to be holy.

Here we have Scripture on top of Scripture. Peter quotes from the Old Testament (Lev. 11:44): "For the scripture says, 'You must be holy, because I am holy' " (1 Peter 1: 16, TEV).

You Have Been Ransomed

I heard Dr. E. S. James tell a moving story about a boy out of the long ago. The boy built a boat which he often floated in the stream back of his house. One day he placed the boat in the stream, tied a string to the bank, and left for a while. When he returned, the string had broken, and the beloved boat was gone. His heart was broken.

One day the boy was walking along the street when a toy boat in a pawnshop caught his eye. Upon closer examination he recognized it as his own creation. The boat had floated down the stream and finally drifted to the shore of the Thames where somebody had found it and left it at the pawnshop.

The boy inquired as to the ransom price and bought the boat back. On the way home, holding the beloved boat close to his body, the boy said, "Now you are twice mine. You are mine because I made you. You are mine again because I bought you."

We are the Lord's because he created us. We became lost, and he bought us back. Isn't this a high enough motive to make us live better?

"For you know what was paid to set you free from the worthless manner of life you received from your ancestors. It was not something that loses its value, such as silver or gold; you were set free by the costly sacrifice of Christ, who was like a lamb without defect or spot. He had been chosen by God before the creation of the world, and was revealed in these last days for your sake. Through him you believe in God, who raised him from death and gave him glory; and so your faith and hope are fixed on God" (1:18-21, TEV).

You Are Permanently Changed

There is not much that is permanent in this world. Businesses fail, bodies are broken, homes go on the rocks, educational institutions totter, empires fall, and religious systems rot on the vine.

A man who had built a financial empire stood by the grave of his sinful son and said, "I detest every dollar I have ever made. I'd give every cent to have one more chance with my son."

That which seems so important now will be so unimportant one day. That which looks most appetizing today will be garbage tomorrow.

Is anything permanent? Is anything a sure thing?

All men are like wild grass,
And all their glory is like its flower;
The grass dies, and its flower falls off,
But the word of the Lord remains forever.

When you are born again, you never die. "I give them eternal life, and they shall never die; and no one can snatch them away from me. What my Father has given me is greater than all, and no one can snatch them away from the Father's care" (John 10:28,29, TEV).

"Who, then, can separate us from the love of Christ? Can trouble do it, or hardship, or persecution, or hunger, or poverty, or danger, or death? As the scripture says,

> 'For your sake we are in danger of death the whole day long,
> We are treated like sheep that are going to be slaughtered.'

"No, in all these things we have complete victory through him who loved us! For I am certain that nothing can separate us from his love: neither death nor life; neither angels nor other heavenly rulers or powers; neither the present nor the future; neither the world above nor the world below—there is nothing in all creation that will ever be able to separate us from the love of God which is ours through Christ Jesus our Lord" (Rom. 8:35-39, TEV).

Here is something permanent. No wonder we are admonished to holy living. Can you think of a higher incentive? "For through the living and eternal word of God you have been born again as the children of a parent who is immortal, not mortal" (1 Peter 1:23, TEV).

You Are in a Holy Fellowship

Everybody likes to "belong." Nobody wants to be left out. Purpose is added to our lives if we are a part of something important. These high incentives have sometimes been perverted to destructive and unholy causes. Hitler appealed to these high instincts for his own selfish ends. Communism has achieved unusual success in perverting God-given instincts to self-destructive and satanic ends. There is nothing new about this. This was the method of Satan in the Garden. Praise God, he failed with Jesus in the wilderness.

One of the highest motives to holiness is that we belong to something high and holy. We are living stones in a living spiritual temple. We "serve as holy priests, to offer spiritual and acceptable sacrifices to God through Jesus Christ" (1 Peter 2:5, TEV).

Do you sometimes wonder if the church critics really know what the church is? I am writing these words while involved in a gigantic evangelistic crusade. More than seventy churches in this geographic area are engaged in special evangelistic efforts this week. Less than three hours ago, I heard a man emphasizing "going where the people are." He was correct in giving this emphasis. He was incorrect in implying that he is doing what the church is not doing. If he is going in the name of Jesus, he is the church going. If we go for self-glory, it is neither Jesus nor his church.

A New Testament church is not a building. A church may be in or out of a building. There is nothing wrong about a church having meetings in a building. There is nothing right about confining the church to a building. The church is God's people worshiping God and letting God work through them wherever they are.

Here is where we church members must begin. We must come to God. When we see him in his holiness, power, and love we can begin to see ourselves. We have a tendency to look in the mirror and then turn away, forgetting what we look like (James 1:24).

Are there some sins down in the basement of your life? You have tried to forget them, but every so often you are reminded. These sins, like slimy reptiles, do all right in the dark. They are protected. The trouble is that, occasionally, the lid is lifted and you smell the stench of them. They may even crawl out and cause you some embarrassment. These are not sins other people usually know about. They are sins of the spirit mostly. Let the light in. Confess your sin. Ask God to forgive you and make you clean.

Being members of the Lord's body should inspire a desire for holiness. Being living stones in God's temple should challenge us. Praise God for the privilege of being in a New Testament church. I am one among many stones, but every stone of whatever shape and design is important. I am thankful for the Chief Cornerstone and its stability, else the building long ago would have fallen.

"But you are the chosen race, the King's priests, the holy nation, God's own people, chosen to proclaim the wonderful acts of God, who called you from the darkness into his own marvelous light. At one time you were not God's people, but now you are his people; at one time you did not know God's mercy, but now you have received his mercy" (1 Peter 2:9,10, TEV).

Be holy!

11

How to Be Humble

A sales manager was approached by several girls selling Brownie cookies. They offered no sales pitch, so he began questioning them to see if they could develop one. "Why do you want to see me?" he asked.

One little girl piped up: "Because you are so handsome."

He couldn't resist the argument. He bought six boxes. "There are no better sales tools," he said, "than truth and honesty."

Peter wrote, "Be clothed with humility: for God resisteth the proud, and giveth grace to the humble. Humble yourselves therefore under the mighty hand of God, that he may exalt you in due time: Casting all your care upon him; for he careth for you" (1 Peter 5:5-7).

Peter is expressing the same mandate to humility which is everywhere evident in the Bible. In the above passage he not only expresses a mandate but makes clear a motive to humility, which is promised blessings from God. Since humility is living in deference to others instead of directing attention to oneself, Peter points out that humility, like other Christian virtues, depends upon our faith in God: "Casting all your care upon him; for he careth for you."

Humility is a rather strange word in our day of flights to other planets and international "negotiations from power." Yet, there is a sense in which it is all the more important and appropriate. After all, humility and weakness are not synonymous terms. Rather, the reverse is true. Humility is not emphasizing how weak and unworthy we are. It is surrendering ourselves to the power of Christ through whom we receive strength for all things.

Humility as a Citizen

At no time since the American Revolution has there been so much rebellion against authority in America. It is not against one institution but all institutions which represent authority. This is understandable, because disrespect and rebellion are very contagious. If children in the home hear their parents criticizing the government, politicians, preachers, teachers and all others who represent authority, it is only natural that this same spirit and attitude will be caught by the children. They, of course, will include parents in their list because they represent authority also.

In Peter's day totalitarianism was the rule, and rulers were often corrupt and sensual. They demanded complete worship as well as obedience. Some Christians died rather than worship them—perhaps some to whom Peter wrote. Yet it was not becoming to Christian discipleship to misuse one's freedom. Had these early Christians used all their energies to correct the social and political evils of their day, we would never have had a New Testament.

There are many social inequities in our day. Some church members are blind to them and some even concur in them. There is much political corruption, and the participants are usually church members. Most church members, however, do not participate in politics and social action—except to criticize.

Some seem to feel that the main purpose of elected officials is to provide a target for criticism. One often wonders if most of the poison arrows of criticism are not guilt-inspired. The Christian leader must never be afraid to express himself on political and social issues; neither is this to be his main business.

It is a mark of Christian humility to be a law-abiding citizen with proper respect for all authority from constable to president. It is a mark of Christian humility to go to the polls and vote (sometimes to run for office). The humble Christian then prays that God will intervene and use the elected candidate for his purposes.

America still enjoys unique freedom of expression. Christians must respond with responsibility. Humility is not to be used as an escape from responsibility.

The best thing a Christian can do for his country is to pray; that is, if he believes God's promises. If he prays maturely, the other responses will be mature.

Humility Where You Work

Christianity, with its regard for human worth, has made an immeasurable contribution to the working man. While Jesus may not often get the credit, a study of history will reveal this truth. Slavery, child labor, sweatshops, poor pay, and racial discrimination cannot continue to exist in a Christ-oriented society. The humble Christian will praise God for achievements in these areas and dedicate himself to more advanced goals.

There is another side to the coin, however. The Bible has something to say to the employee. Peter makes the point against a background of extremes. If a slave can act like a Christian, how much more obligated are those under more favorable circumstances?

"You servants must submit yourselves to your masters and show them complete respect, not only to those who are kind and considerate, but also to those who are harsh. God will bless you for this, if you endure the pain of unjust suffering because you are conscious of his will. For what credit is there in enduring the beatings you deserve for having done wrong? But if you endure suffering even when you have done right, God will bless you for it" (vv. 18-20).

Peter is not defending slavery, but is speaking of Christian conduct, even for a slave. While the influence of Jesus has been felt in better working conditions and better pay, it will also be expressed in terms of better attitudes and better work. The Christian displays humility when he acts like a Christian wherever he is.

Some of you, employers and employees, have wonderful Christian relations with each other. I saw this demonstrated often as a pastor visiting businesses where our church had members in all categories. It was easy to sense Christian brotherhood.

Not too long ago I worked in a revival in a small city

with several factories. The pastor made appointments with management for himself and the evangelist to visit these plants (I am not saying this ought always be revival procedure). These managers, sometimes owners, would direct a tour of the place. Sometimes they stopped production in certain areas to introduce personnel, especially if they were members of that church. In several cases the production manager would say something like, "I want to introduce you to this man over here. He is a good man, but he needs the Lord."

In one case the president of the firm said to a mechanic, "Bill, I want you to meet my preacher and the visiting evangelist." After the brief visit he said, "Bill, we are having a roll call of members in our church this week. Tonight is the time for my family to be introduced. All our family names will be called and any special guests of our family. I would like to have you and Elsie and the kids be our guests tonight if you can. My wife sings in the choir. I will take her over early for rehearsal and drive by your house to pick you up."

That is both good labor relations and good evangelism. The Bible, however, teaches that we are to act right even if the other fellow does not.

Humility at Home

Perhaps the truest test of humility is at home. Peter was a family man. Celibacy has its advantages, but a happy marriage seems to have more. Besides, Peter had been brought to Jesus by his brother. He knew firsthand the joyous advantages of Christian family relations.

Peter is writing to wives about winning their husbands.

He is saying it can be done, notwithstanding their social disadvantage. He points out the method is not the world's method.

In the first place women cannot win their husbands to Christ with talk. "It will not be necessary for you to say a word, for they will see how pure and reverent your conduct is" (1 Peter 3:1-2, TEV).

I visited in a home where the wife was a church member in another city. The husband said he was not a Christian. I would have preferred talking with them separately, and especially so after she said, "Get on him. I'd go to church if he would, but I can't be a Christian by myself."

I decided to make the most of the situation and began talking with the man. It was difficult because the wife's contribution was everything but helpful. Wise Christian women often leave the room when someone is witnessing to their husbands. A man can usually be witnessed to with greater effectiveness if you are alone with him.

Notwithstanding the handicap, the husband trusted Jesus as Saviour. The wife said accusingly, "He'll tell you that but he doesn't mean it. He won't be any different."

I said to the woman, "Now let's pray together about your life with the Lord."

"Well, I know I need it," she answered, "but I can't live it by myself." We prayed together in a spirit of love and asked her if she would move her membership and re-dedicate her life that night as her husband made a profession of faith.

"Yes, I'll be glad to, but he won't do it." I was a little surprised that he did.

Peter goes on to say to the Christian women of his day that they cannot win their husbands by merely dressing up and looking pretty. "Instead, your beauty should consist of your true inner self, the ageless beauty of a gentle and quiet spirit, which is of great value in God's sight" (v.4).

Obviously, humility can never be superficial. It grows with Christlikeness. "You husbands, also, in living with your wives you must recognize that they are the weaker sex and so you must treat them with respect; for they also will receive, together with you, God's gift of life. Do this so that nothing will interfere with your prayers" (v.7).

Husbands may be more willing to accept the "weaker sex" line than wives. Emancipation has been successful, to put it mildly. We should remember that this is a contribution of Christianity.

Not long ago I was in South Korea. The Christian faith is gaining ground there very rapidly, but it is not in any sense the predominant religion. Women are also gaining ground commensurately, but they are still in the background socially. In church the men and women sit on opposite sides. A man seldom refers to his wife publicly. When he does, it is usually a joke.

In Korea if a man and wife are seen together in public, he will be in front and the wife will follow. She may have a baby strapped to her back and a heavy load on top of her head.

The story goes of the American who reprimanded the Korean man about these practices. Next time he saw the couple they were coming down a steep incline. The woman had the big load, but sure enough, the woman was in front. The American, happy with that much progress, congratulated the Korean for walking behind his wife.

The Korean responded, "You see there is a danger of

falling down on this steep incline, and I would not want to be in front."

This might help us understand more easily the culture of Peter's day. The teaching is applicable in both cases, however. While women are not inferior in most ways, they are weaker physically. It is a mark of gentlemanliness as well as Christian humility (they never conflict) for the husband to defer to his wife.

There is also the evangelistic note here, "For they also will receive, together with you, God's gift of life" (v. 7).

The next line is a surprise, "Do this so that nothing will interfere with your prayers" (v. 7). The obvious implication is that if husbands do not have the right attitude toward their wives, they will not have the right attitude toward God.

Humility for the Preacher

"I appeal to the church elders among you, I who am an elder myself. I am a witness of Christ's sufferings, and I have a share of the glory which will be revealed" (1 Peter 5:1, TEV).

Peter felt that he had a right to admonish the elders. The late Dr. Norris Gilliam of Tennessee used to say jokingly in addressing pastors, "I like to speak to preachers because they are one of whom I am which."

The pastor role may have lost some of its comparative prestige but it has not lost any of its comparative importance. Glamour and greatness are not synonymous terms anyway.

"I appeal to you" says Peter, "be shepherds of the flock God gave you" (vv. 1,2). What greater appeal could be made? Do we believe that God actually gives a certain flock to a certain shepherd? What a motivation for humility on the part of pastors, pulpit committees, and congregations!

Nothing brings greater strength and dynamic to the preacher than the conviction that God called him. The prophets had the courage to speak against the evils of their day because God called them. Early Christian preachers spoke with boldness at the risk of their lives because God called them. They felt that the proclamation of God's Word was more important than their lives. "Woe is me if I preach not the Gospel."

The answer to God's call has often been a traumatic experience for the preacher. It was true with Isaiah, Jeremiah, Amos, and Ezekiel. It was true with Paul. Like the conversion experience, however, it is less cataclysmic for others, but no less compelling.

Some preachers say that God did not call them. They say they selected their vocation like anybody else. Who would be inclined to argue with them?

One preacher was chiding another for his belief that God had called him. "God doesn't call anybody to preach," he said. "It is the height of egocentricity to make such a claim."

The other preacher smiled and said, "You remind me of a story I heard in childhood. There was a farm laborer who was a devoted Christian. He prayed, read the Bible, and testified all the time, much to the chagrin of his boss. The boss one day said to the laborer, "All this religion stuff is a lot of foolishness. There is no God."

"Please, sir," said the laborer, "just say there ain't no God as far as you know."

Peter's implication is that God not only calls men, but

he calls them to certain responsibilities—"the flock God gave you." Would not this call out of the man the very most in dedication, prayer, study and work? Would this not relieve a man of fear and insecurity about his future?

Be shepherds of the flock and look after it. What a responsibility! What excitement! What a thrill! In this respect a minister fills the role of physician. It is people-centered. People are important to God, and people need Jesus. The people may or may not be aware of their needs. This intensifies the responsibility and humility of the minister.

A faithful minister, now deceased, had this to say in a pastors' conference at Union University thirty years ago: "There is a woman in my church who is a professional troublemaker. She keeps something going all the time. She pesters me to death. I have often found myself saying, 'Wouldn't it be nice to pastor this church without that woman?' Then I remember that she perhaps needs a pastor more than any other member of our church, and I go on trying to help her."

The pastor is a shepherd and not a "little tin god" lording it over his flock. One of the frustrations of the pastorate is how to be a strong leader, and "overseer" without being self-centered and domineering in his posture as pastor. Here is where real humility is essential. Dynamic spiritual leadership is possible only as self is removed. A truly humble person does not "act humble." Weak leadership is not leadership. It is often a self-centered escape from responsibility.

God pity the pastor (and the church) where every decision must be made in terms "of what it will do to me."

This is seldom deliberate but much sadder because it is subconscious.

God pity, also, the fellow who flees responsibility by running to another church if the road gets rough. Genuine humility avoids both pitfalls. The pastorate is not easy. Are any responsible positions easy? Some pastorates should be long; some should be short. The decision belongs to the Holy Spirit.

I praise God for our pastors. Besides having been a pastor myself (I thank God that he gave me this undeserved privilege), I have had more pastors than the average preacher. I have been given the privilege of working with many hundreds of pastors in evangelism. As a whole they are the most unselfish men I have known. To these men I say, "You have been examples to the flock. And when the Chief Shepherd appears, you will receive the glorious crown which will never lose its brightness."

Peter's appeal to humility, faith, and obedience is the example of Christ. All through this discussion Peter refers to the sufferings and death of Jesus. This is evidence of the change that has taken place in Peter's life. We remember that he was the one who so violently opposed the idea that our Lord might have to die and wanted to defend him personally. Now he has learned that it was necessary for Jesus to die in order for us to have eternal life. He is calling upon us to follow the example of Jesus.

12

When Life Begins

Some say, "Life begins at forty." Some men in their forties have hoped it begins at fifty. A spirited old man said, "Life begins at eighty." Ask a doctor when life begins, and he answers scientifically. Ask a child when life begins, and he uninhibitedly answers, "Life begins when you are born." When does life begin?

This book began with a discussion of life: the love of life, the mystery of life, the fight for life. We have discussed strength for living under several topics, but life must have a beginning.

Do you need to come alive? How would you like to have born in you a brand new person who will be happier, better-adjusted, more productive, easier to get along with, less sinful and selfish than you have ever imagined anybody could be? How would you like to live in this world of space and time, change and decay, fear and worry, sin and defeat, and at the same time be in such touch with eternity that you are exactly the kind of person God meant for you to be?

This is what God desires for you: "By his own will he brought us into being through the word of truth, so that we should occupy first place among all his creatures" (James 1:18, TEV).

Normal, healthy-minded people desire this kind of life. They know they don't have it and may feel that the realization of it is beyond reach. Now I ask, Why would God place the desire there if it is unattainable? Thirst assumes there is water somewhere. Hunger assumes there is food somewhere. The capacity to love assumes that there is a person somewhere who will respond to that love.

Nearly two thousand years ago, a man walked out into the night under the compulsion of that desire. His life had been touched by a strange, mysterious Person whom he thought might answer his questions. The result: he found answers to questions he was incapable of asking. He found what he needed without knowing he needed it. Nicodemus came to Jesus for a discussion and left—a new man.

Who Needs It?

Nicodemus did not come running to Jesus saying, "Good Teacher, what must I do to inherit eternal life?" Nicodemus was not a leper, not a cripple, not blind, not a tax collector and not poor. Nicodemus was "well fixed." He was "in."

In a town where I used to be pastor, there was a community appropriately named "Needmore." Nicodemus did not live in Needmore.

He was a member of the "right church." In fact, "the only church." The typical Jew knew that nobody but a Jew was in the kingdom and was rather glad of it. Do you know

Gentiles like that? Nicodemus was not only a Hebrew, he was a very special kind of Hebrew. He was a Pharisee. They were the best people in the world. No knowledgeable person would argue the question.

The Pharisees were keepers of the law. They knew the first five books of the Old Testament backwards and forwards. They observed all the precepts meticulously and to the letter. This was not all. Since these writings were the "law," they had to cover everything. There had to be an answer for every question and a precept for every situation. The scribes had filled it in. Thousands of columns had been written. For example, there was a commandment about Sabbath observance. The equivalent of dozens of books were written so that everybody could have a law to fit every detail of his life in regard to the Sabbath.

Wherever there are laws, there are loopholes. So, many pages were written covering loopholes. It was a violation of the law to tie a knot on the Sabbath. However, a knot that could be tied with one hand was allowable. One's dexterity might determine what he could do on the Sabbath. Also, one's ingenuity might give him license. For example, it was wrong to tie a knot in a rope and draw a bucket of water, but it was not wrong to tie certain knots in women's clothing. Why not use a piece of clothing to draw water?

The Pharisees had to know all these laws and keep them. They were very special people, and it is easy to understand that there were never more than six thousand of them. Nicodemus was a Pharisee.

Furthermore, he was a sophisticated Pharisee. He was a member of the Sanhedrin. He was on the executive board and the administrative committee of his denomination. He was a combination of theological professor and supreme court judge. That he was a man of wealth was indicated by the gifts he brought to Jesus' burial.

What did Nicodemus need? Jesus told him he needed to be born again. Here was a man who was supposed to be in the top echelon of the popular view of the kingdom. But Jesus told him he would have to be born again to even see the kingdom.

Because man is sinful by nature, he is incapable of perceiving the spiritual life. Because he was born in sin, he must be born of the Spirit. Perhaps the most common error in the name of Christianity is the notion that one is a Christian if he is a reasonably good man. The most frequent excuse the witness encounters is "I'm not a bad fellow. I live the best I can, what more can I do?" Again, "I live as well as most of the church members I know"; or, "I'm afraid I can't live up to it."

My wife teaches a class of young married women in the church. Recently a Panamanian member of her class trusted Jesus as Saviour. She insisted that she be given a set of rules to follow. "Please tell me what I can do and what I can't do. I don't want to make any mistakes." My wife gave her a Bible.

"But," she said, "I want to know what a Baptist can do and what he can't do."

Many faithful church members expect the preacher to play the scribe and make a rule book for the Bible. Some preachers try to comply!

It is difficult to "see" the kingdom of God. Only those who enter can see, and one cannot enter without becoming a new person. If anybody could enter the kingdom without a new birth, Nicodemus could.

There is a widely popular view that everybody has a right to his own religious beliefs and it really doesn't make any difference just so one is sincere. "We are headed for the same place," they say. It is difficult to imagine two people headed for the same place by going in opposite directions.

Admittedly, the Christian religion is very narrow. Christians don't make it that way. Jesus does! Jesus said, "I am the way, I am the truth, I am the life; no one goes to the Father except by me" (John 14:6, TEV). "I tell you the truth that no one can enter the Kingdom of God unless he is born of water and the Spirit" (John 3:5, TEV).

The secretary of evangelism for a large denomination asked in an evangelism conference: "Do you think only Christians will be saved? What about the Hindu, the Buddhist, the Mohammedan? Don't we think God loves them too?" Yes, he does. That is the reason he gave his only begotten Son, that whoever believes in him should not perish, but have everlasting life.

Who Wants It?

We have already pointed out that Nicodemus did not come running to Jesus asking the way of eternal life. The one who did, went away without it. Yet, Nicodemus must have known he needed something. As a Pharisee he had gone as far as he could in his religion, but he still felt empty. Normal people everywhere feel a void and long for a full life. You may have seen people worship idols. Why would one bow down before a god of brass or iron or wood or gold? He goes to the shrine and worships, hoping it will help his hollow inadequacy.

The religion of Nicodemus recognized the one true God,

but the system had deteriorated to the point where it was a burdensome load of empty jars that held no water. "For my people have committed two evils; they have forsaken me the fountain of living waters, and hewed them out cisterns, broken cisterns, that can hold no water" (Jer. 2:13). Why do people try to drink from empty churns that hold no water? They are thirsty and have not found the well of water springing up into eternal life.

If Nicodemus had discovered the emptiness of his religion, why did he come to Jesus by night? Who knows? Maybe it was his first opportunity to have a personal conference with Jesus. But even if he was seeking him secretly, which is likely—what is so bad about that? Do you sometimes go to some secret place and kneel to pray? Is it because you are ashamed or afraid?

What is still more likely is that he was not satisfied with his own religion, and he was not yet sure about Jesus. Let us be glad he came at all. Most of his kind did not and do not. Perhaps many of his colleagues had been impressed with Jesus. "While Jesus was in Jerusalem during the Passover Feast, many believed in him as they saw the mighty works he did" (John 2:23, TEV). Nicodemus said, "We know, Rabbi, that you are a teacher sent by God. No one could do the mighty works you are doing unless God were with him" (John 3:2, TEV). He spoke in the plural. He and other religious leaders had likely had many discussions about him. Nicodemus must have had more courage than any of the others. It should be noted that there is no recorded complaint from Jesus about Nicodemus coming by night.

Aren't we glad Jesus is willing to allow any of us an audience day or night? The Samaritan woman came to a well where he was resting. The crowds often sought him out when he had gone aside to rest or pray. A government official in Capernaum knew he needed Jesus to heal his son. He went to Cana and called on Jesus to help him. I have called on him at some pretty awful hours, haven't you?

A few days ago I talked with a Hawaiian woman who sat beside me on a plane to Tokyo. She was making her first trip to Japan to attend her brother's funeral in Okinawa. She confided that her Buddhist religion did not satisfy her. What she really wants is new life which can come only through Christ.

I spoke on a recent Sunday to an English-speaking group at the Baptist Hospital in Pusan, Korea. Two people trusted Jesus as Saviour, one of them Korean and the other an American seaman. Several others indicated their desire, but they did not make a full surrender. When they learned we were to have another service later in the morning, they came across town to attend the service in a church. Some of them were saved there.

There are nearly twenty-eight million people in Korea who do not claim to be Christians. Everywhere, they seem to sense their need. What they really want is new life. They are thirsty, but are seeking to satisfy this thirst from the broken churns of business success, social recognition, scientific achievement, bodily lust, and a thousand kinds of entertainment.

"Do not be surprised because I tell you, 'you must all be born again' " (John 3:7, TEV).

Who Can Have It?

"How can a grown man be born again?" Nicodemus

should not have been so naive. He was a doctor of Old Testament theology, and the prophets spoke of the need for new life. "A new heart also will I give you, and a new spirit will I put within you" (Ezek. 36:26).

The vision of the valley of dry bones was a reminder that God can perform the miracle of bringing life where there is only death. Many who know they have a need for new life are not willing to pay the price of complete surrender. They do not wish to openly refuse it, so they claim they cannot understand it.

You can more easily sympathize with a person who has no religious background whatever. But here is a preacher who wants to literalize about the impossibility of going back to his mother's womb to be born a second time. Some religious leaders of our day are very critical of literalism, until they need a defense for unspirituality. They then sound like Nicodemus. Many very orthodox brothers always keep a safe distance from the Spirit-filled life. Tradition and public opinion are very dear. To die to self is too expensive even to receive the new life.

Jesus made it very clear to Nicodemus that new life is available to those who are willing to pay the price of breaking from pride, position, and tradition. John the Baptist had made it clear that being a son of Abraham was not enough. But self would have to die before Nicodemus would be willing to submit openly to Christian baptism. Jesus called for an open confession. This public confession was expressed by baptism. This would be a real test for Nicodemus.

A man who had been attending services regularly was visited by the pastor. The preacher talked with him about his personal relationship with the Lord.

The man said, "Yes, I know what you mean. I have trusted Jesus. My sins have been forgiven and I want to join your church." He went on, "You know, Preacher, it's a funny thing. I've been planning to call you. Since I've been saved, I know I need to be baptized. So I thought I'd just call you up some night when you are not very busy, and we would meet down at the church house and you could baptize me." Nicodemus might have been more interested in that approach. There is really no such thing, however, as a secret disciple. This is as unrealistic as secret weddings. Both involve complete commitment.

Of course the "nitty gritty" (as the kids say) was the birth of the Spirit. Jesus made it clear that Nicodemus could be born from above even though he did not understand it.

One can witness and experience the effects of the wind without understanding it. This illustration by Jesus is more interesting when we remember that the same word is used for "wind" and for "Spirit" in several languages, including the Greek and Hebrew. One can breathe the air, enjoy the cool breeze, sail a boat, fly a kite or witness a tornado without understanding the wind.

One can be born of the Spirit, be filled with the Spirit, live by the Spirit, and be empowered by the Spirit without understanding the Spirit.

I am not trying to put a premium on ignorance, but we benefit daily by many things we do not understand. My brother, brother-in-law, and three nephews are in the electrical business. They understand far more about electronics than I, but a hundred-watt bulb gives me as much light as it does them.

"How can these things be?" asked Nicodemus. Jesus reminded him that they had been talking about very simple things and if they were still hazy to the great teacher, how much more his difficulty in receiving these great heavenly truths. The truth is that Nicodemus felt at home in religious discussion. You have perhaps tried to witness to people who enjoyed the discussion as long as it was just discussion.

Jesus never seemed to have too much time to spend in idle talk. One day he and his disciples saw a blind man, and the disciples asked Jesus whose sin was responsible for his blindness, the man's or his parents'? Jesus told them that it was neither. But he did remind them of the importance of doing the work of God while it is day, because the night is coming. He then healed the blind man. Healing him is much more important than discussing him.

They say the Pharisees and scribes spent a lot of time in such discussion: "Since angels are not spatial, how many angels can dance on the point of a needle?"

Medical men may spend some time discussing theories of disease and treatment, but the time comes when the sick must be treated. Reading and exchanging recipes is wonderful, but only the food satisfies hunger.

Jesus had time and patience to work with Nicodemus, but he was not willing to waste his time and Nicodemus' soul with theological play.

With his patient determination Jesus continued by illustrating again how unnecessary it is to understand the new life in order to receive it. He recalled an experience in Hebrew history with which all religious leaders were entirely familiar. He reminded Nicodemus of the time when the children of Israel had sinned in the wilderness and were punished by an infestation of poisonous serpents. The people, as they always did, came to Moses for help. Moses, as he always did, went to God in intercession for

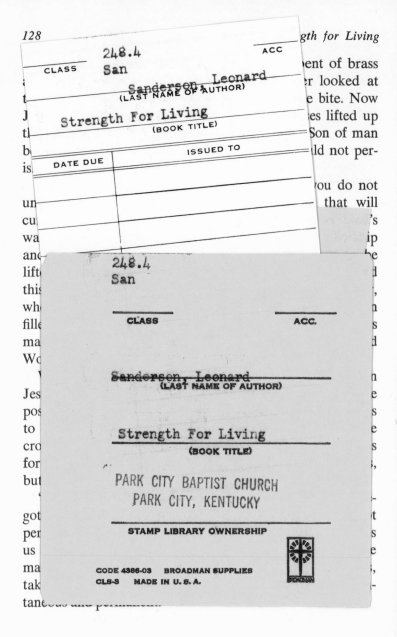

ent of brass
er looked at
e bite. Now
es lifted up
Son of man
ld not per-

ou do not
that will

un
cu
wa
an
lift
this
wh
fille
ma
Wo

Jes
pos
to
cro
for
but

got
per
us
ma
tak
taneous and permanent.